A THEOLOGY OF THE LAITY

Books by
HENDRIK KRAEMER
Published by The Westminster Press

A THEOLOGY OF THE LAITY
RELIGION AND THE CHRISTIAN FAITH
THE COMMUNICATION OF THE CHRISTIAN FAITH

A THEOLOGY

OF

THE LAITY

by

Hendrik Kraemer

Philadelphia

THE WESTMINSTER PRESS

Library of Congress Catalog Card No. 59–6251

TYPESET IN GREAT BRITAIN

PRINTED IN THE UNITED STATES OF AMERICA

CONTENTS

5

19879

FOREWORD

THIS little book contains, in extended form, what I said on " A Theology of the Laity " in the Hulsean Lectures at Cambridge, between February 17th and 28th, 1958. The same should have been presented in the Gunning Lectures at New College, Edinburgh, between March 10th and 14th, 1958, but illness prevented me from giving more than one lecture.

I take the opportunity of expressing my sincere thanks to the Trustees of both series of lectures for having conferred on me the honour of being a Hulsean and Gunning Lecturer.

In particular I feel the need to express my gratitude to Dr. and Mrs. R. D. Whitehorn at Cambridge, who kindly extended to me the hospitality of Westminster College, for their many personal attentions, and not less to Dr. and Mrs. W. S. Tindal at Edinburgh for their generous friendship. I will always remember with gratitude the opportunity I had in the Royal Infirmary at Edinburgh, of making the acquaintance of the National Health Service of Great Britain and being the object of the excellent care of its doctors and nurses.

H. KRAEMER.

INTRODUCTORY OBSERVATIONS

I T I S M Y experience that prefaces, generally speaking, are not really read, however pertinent they may and should be for a right judgment on the subject matter of the book. Therefore I open this book with a short chapter of introductory observations. These observations are essential for the understanding of the inner urge, the peculiar vision and the specific historic situation which are behind the following chapters.

The theme of this book, " A Theology of the Laity ", calls with great emphasis for treatment in the present condition of the Christian Churches all over the world. It is even more adequate to say, it cries for treatment. For reasons of principle and of practical relevance.

The laity or the body of lay-membership of the Church has never in Church History enjoyed the distinction of being treated with care and thoroughness as a matter of specific theological importance or significance. It has been dismissed in passing, by stray remarks or in generalities as e.g. the universal priesthood of believers. The theologians, especially since the days of the 16th century Reformation, have addressed themselves with great zeal and ability to a theological motivation of the training, preparation, function and status of the Ministry, that is to say, the ordained and consecrated Clergy. This is all to the good, because it is a necessary and indispensable part of a coherent doctrine of the Church. This statement about exclusive theological attention to the Ministry or Clergy holds true in regard to both types of Churches: the Episcopal

9

and non-episcopal. Even in the present ecumenical discussion on the understanding of the Church, in so far as it happens under the auspices and direction of "Faith and Order", it is striking to find that "Faith and Order", quite rightly demanding a renewed attempt at an ecumenical understanding of the Ministry of the Church, evidently thinks only about Ministry in terms of the Clergy or the body of ordained Ministers. It is striking, because it seems as if the Department of Faith and Order is unaware of the thinking and searching which is going on in its sister-department in the World Council of Churches, the Department of the Laity.

As far as I can see, this subsidiary treatment or great neglect, by the professional theologians, of the laity as a distinct part of the full scope of the Church, as to its theological place or "locus", is an inexcusable lack and an indication of a partly mis-orientated understanding of the Church in its wholeness. It is true that, as we will have opportunity to note repeatedly in the following chapters, in the last decades a steadily increasing amount of literature has appeared and is appearing, on the place, the significance and the responsibility of the lay-membership of the Church(es), as a concomitant of the growing appeal to the laity for their commitment to the task of the Church. This literature is mostly practical, but contains also many valuable short theological thrusts or apercu's. Yet a systematic attempt at a theological foundation and motivation of the laity's place and meaning, as inherent in the nature and calling of the Church, has not so far been undertaken. At least, in the non-Roman part of the "Christian" world. This little book intends to be a modest attempt and contribution towards a real theology of the Laity.

We must acknowledge with all due humility that in

this respect our Roman Catholic brethren are ahead of us non-Roman Christians. In 1953 the well-known Father Yves M. J. Congar published a book entitled: *Jalons pour une théologie du laïcat*. It is significant that Congar calls his voluminous book, packed with theological erudition of high calibre, nevertheless *jalons*, that is to say, rough headings or first attempts. He is duly conscious of the novelty of the undertaking and, consequently, does not claim to present a definitive treatment. Neither do I with my more modestly-sized attempt. On page 7 of the "Introduction" he formulates his theme in a characteristically Roman Catholic way, nevertheless impelled by the dynamic present circumstances to treat it in a new setting. His words are: "Les laïcs formeront toujours dans l'Eglise un ordre subordonné (! K.), mais ils sont en train de retrouver une plus pleine conscience d'en être organiquement des membres actifs, de plein droit et de plein exercice."[1]

Congar's aim manifestly is to break through the opportunistic or pragmatic motivation of the powerful "Action Catholique" through the whole Roman Catholic world, and to provide a theological basis for it. We are quite at one with him in his concern for a theological definition of the place, the responsibility and the function of the laity as a great component of the body of the Church, and also with his conviction that such a theological definition is an imperious demand for a fuller understanding of the Church and for a more

---

[1] "Lay people will always form a subordinate (! K.) order in the Church, but they are in process of recovering a fuller consciousness of being organically active members of it, with full rights and full performance." An English translation of this book, *Lay People in the Church*, appeared in 1957.

adequate discharge of the task of the Church in the world of to-day. This concern and this conviction constitute the reason of principle for a theology of the laity to which we have alluded already. A theology *of* the laity, not *for* the laity. These two have to be clearly distinguished. The matter of a theology *for* the laity, that is, the kind and amount of theological information necessary for lay-people, is very important, but it should not be confused with a theology *of* the Laity. It is part of the consequences to be derived from a Theology *of* the Laity as expression of the Church's spiritual strategy, when it has seized the point of a theology of the laity.

In itself the reason of principle, that is to say the formulation of more adequate understanding of the Church as it is meant in the biblical revelation, is quite sufficient to justify the attempt towards a theological motivation of the specific place and calling of the lay-membership of the Church(es). Universal experience, however, proves that the prevailing inertness of human nature, also in the Church, makes it in most cases necessary that an incentive from outside compel us to see and seize what is inherent in the verities by which we theoretically live. The Church is no exception to this rule. Repeatedly in history, by the great impetus issuing from social, political and cultural upheavals outside, the Church has been compelled to *re*discover its own faith and God's purpose in Jesus Christ, and to *re*interpret it and its implications. Outside incentives of this kind have become especially operative during and after the Second World War, and have led, for reasons which will later on be discussed, to a new prominence of the laity, in the considerations and activities of the Churches. Especially has the growing recognition, in many Churches, of their evangelistic or missionary responsibility to their environment, contributed a great deal to this new prominence.

Everywhere in the world there is evident in many Churches a new outburst of lay-participation and activity, or, at least, a growing concern about it. The lay issue has become, if one compares the Ecumenical Assembly at Amsterdam with that of Evanston and the post-Evanston period, a central object of interest in the World Council of Churches. The special Lay-Conferences of Bad Boll (1951) and Buffalo (1952) are evidence of the same trend. Lay-movements, big and small, mushroom all over the place. The most significant lay-movement in the non-Roman world, the "Kirchentag" in Germany, has great promise, if it maintains its ecumenical vision. There is going on a constant prodding of the laity out of their passivity and their spectator-attitude. Efforts towards what is called "mobilization" of the laity and special training and activating occur in many places. In certain countries, especially European countries and Great Britain, a new category of men, fully absorbed in their secular professions, are at the same time active and vocal as lay-theologians. Phrases such as "the ministry of the laity", though often not really understood, are becoming current.

We will return to this whole trend in its various ramifications. These few remarks only want, by way of introduction, to stress the practical relevance of the laity-issue in present-day Church life. This book is written from the conviction that all this new activity, experiment and searching, which in so many respects evokes much gratitude and joy, will ultimately fail if it has no lasting and serious theological foundation. It will appear in the future mere temporary effervescence or a passing eruption of activism, without real backbone, if it is not undergirded by a well-thought-out theology of the laity on a biblical basis, which becomes a natural and inalienable part of that new common understanding of the .Church, the search for which is one of the crucial (if not *the* crucial) elements of the great ecumenical quest. The laity, well considered in the context of a wider, deeper and more dynamic understanding of the Church such as there never was before, is not a body that in times of emergency can be called upon as an auxiliary army, and then dropped when the period of emergency is past. In fact, however, whether conscious or not, this is the prevailing attitude and conception. The purpose of this book is to point in a quite different, more fundamental direction.

The structure of this book is clearly divided into two parts. The first two chapters approach the subject in a purely pragmatic and historical way, without trying to be in any way exhaustive or complete. In these chapters the terms "lay" and "laity" are used in a provisional way, that is to say in the sense of the ordinary member of the Church. In the second chapter we will keep in the main to this wide, undifferentiated sense, but try, in some historical observations, to clarify how the Churches in the course of history have theoretically or practically defined or conceived of the status of the laity in the Church. These pragmatic chapters are, in the writer's opinion, necessary, not because they are wholly new as to information, but because, for a full picture of the lay issue, one must elucidate the factors which in the present situation combine in pressing the attention towards a fundamental rethinking of the place and responsibility of the laity in the Church and in the world, and give an idea in what direction history has moulded the general mood and attitude of the laity as part of the Church. Only by taking these aspects seriously into account is it possible to demonstrate that an attempt at a genuine theology of the laity is not a theoretical matter of fine theological concepts, but an exceedingly practical act, as good thinking or a good theory always is, because it is the sustaining source of informed, spiritually intelligent action.

The third and fourth chapters try to pave the way for the sketch of a Theology of the Laity, contained in the fifth chapter. The Postlude to the outlined Theology of the Laity simply enumerates, in a very succinct way, the manifold and arduous tasks which are implied in making the words " the ministry of the laity " effective.

Chapter 1

THE SIGNS OF THE TIME

FATHER CONGAR opens his book *Jalons pour une théologie du laïcat* by recording a delightful anecdote contained in a conversation between a Cardinal and a priest, in order to illustrate the theoretical and practical insignificance of the laity in the Roman Catholic Church, as reflected in public Roman Catholic opinion. He also does not hesitate to recognize, a few pages further on, that the place of the laity in Roman Catholic Law "est assez petite",[1] which is a rather mitigated description of the result to which his screening of the "Corpus Juris Canonici" has led him. He states clearly that the Corpus is the law of a Church structure which is wholly priestly-hierarchical.

Leaving aside for the moment the various ways in which the non-Roman Churches have defined the place of the laity, or the ways in which the laity has conceived of itself, it is also in the world of non-Roman Churches, generally speaking, true that the Church means in public opinion mainly the Ministry or Clergy. As a consequence of this climate of thinking the laity in the Churches regards itself as of minor and subsidiary significance. Non-Church people share this impression. The reasons are obvious. Representatives of the Ministry figure, by the nature of the case, as the rulers and administrators of the Church, to the public eye. They are, as a rule, the spokesmen of the Church, or are considered to be the really authentic spokesmen. This

[1] *Op. cit.*, p. 11.

17

widespread notion amounts to effectively hiding the practical significance the laity often has, whether acknowledged or not, in the life and witness of the Church. It inclines people, when for some reason the subject of the laity is especially treated, to have a *too* exclusive interest in the "status" of the laity in the Church and to ignore the undeniable fact that in the course of Church History laymen and laywomen, in short the laity, have often played an important rôle.[1]

In order to realize this fact, and so to get things into a somewhat better perspective, it is not superfluous to call back to memory various examples of this importance before we enter into a more special consideration of the many evidences at present of a new importance of the lay issue in the Churches, which need really be envisaged as "Signs of the Time". In order to avoid misunderstanding, we state emphatically that this is not done to glorify or exalt the laity or formulate on behalf of them a "j'accuse" against the official leadership of the Church, but simply as a possibly helpful reminder of facts, too often forgotten, and so resulting in a distorted picture of the Church.

Neither do we mean to labour the obvious fact that in all ages and circumstances the laity by its sheer existence, its more or less faithful participation in the life and work of the Church, and by its more or less obedient reception of the Church's pastoral guidance, is a very substantial phenomenon. Our point is not

---

[1] A good instance of this tendency to think in terms of "status" is the article "Laity" in Hastings' *Encyclopaedia of Religion and Ethics*. It is an article packed with accurate information, and scholarly. Yet marred by two defects: it concerns itself only with the "ecclesiastical" place of the laity, and takes only the Patristic period and English ecclesiastical life into consideration.

to look at the laity as *objects*, but as *subjects* and *agents*. Modern research has made it quite clear that the twelve Apostles occupied in the Church, when it began its career, a quite unique, unrepeatable position, which can neither properly be subsumed under what we have learnt to term the Ministry, nor under the Laity in its technical sense. As to their peculiar place, they had no successors because they were specifically called by Jesus to be witnesses to His Resurrection and His emissaries to evangelize the world. Keeping this in mind, it is significant that with the partial exception of Paul (whose equivalent apostleship was founded in his meeting with Christ on the way to Damascus and his peculiar calling to be the missionary to the Gentiles) the simple lay-character of the Apostles is clearly evident. At the time when they were "pupils" and "followers" of the Master and Lord Jesus, they were called out of simple "secular" occupations. After the Crucifixion a number of them appear to have returned to their "secular" occupation. In Acts 4 : 13 it is quietly stated that the meeting of priests and scribes were astonished about the outspoken witness of Peter and John, the more so because they were uncultured (*agrammatoi*) and common (*idiotai*) people. The Christian Church started its course through the witness and activity of "common" men. Observing that in the New Testament (cf. esp. 1 Cor. 12) the "diakonia" or "ministry" (in the non-technical sense) was to such a great extent charismatic, we may confidently derive from it that many apostles, prophets, teachers, evangelists, etc. (cf. Eph. 4 : 11) were lay-people. Most of the companions of Paul were dedicated lay-people. Women as well as men were such lay "ministers" (cf. Acts 18 : 26; 21 : 9; Rom. 16). The New Testament deals mainly with functions and vocations, not with "offices" as a rule. This implies a prominent rôle of lay-people in the life and witness of the Church.[1]

LAITY IN HISTORY

It is not ·at all new to state these facts. Yet it is necessary because our ordinary perspective is so strongly determined by our Church structures as they have grown in history, and by our system of well-graded "offices" with their neatly defined rights, that a constant reminder of these patent facts is indispensable for a vision of what a living Church is. Therefore it is also not superfluous to accentuate the fact, which is often slurred over without any evil intention, that the expansion of the faith and of the Church in the first centuries mainly happened through the unrecorded witness of the ordinary membership, i.e. the laity, by their word and their way of life. A true exemplification of Roland Allen's *The Spontaneous Expansion of the Church*. Related to this aspect of the primitive Church and of the first three centuries is the rarely realized fact that a number of the great Church Fathers, the first prominent theological thinkers on behalf of the Church, were laymen of great ability. To mention only a few of the very prominent: Tertullian, Cyprian, Augustine. Cyprian and Augustine, having become bishops so to speak by surprise, were essentially, by their whole education and long "secular" career, laymen. The reason why such an obvious fact has to be stated expressly is that their position as Church Fathers has put them so forcefully in the theological, i.e. non-lay, category that the simple

[1] Cf. *The Ministry in Historical Perspective*, edited by H. Richard Niebuhr and Daniel D. Williams, 1956.

truth of their being thinking Christian laymen is entirely forgotten or ignored.

From the 4th century on and through the whole mediaeval period the monastic movement in its different forms (Eastern and Western) and organizations played a prominent part in the life of the Church. We will look at it only from the standpoint of the significance of the laity, apart from its "status". Although the monastic movement did, after its first beginnings, become thoroughly integrated in the hierarchical structure of the Church, and monks became the "regular clergy" in contradistinction to the "secular clergy", its origins and by-products reflect a great amount of lay initiative and lay activity. Congar[1] expresses it very clearly in saying that the monk's condition is, essentially, not defined by his ministry of the "sacred" things, which is the office of the clergy. The first monks in the East had even no liturgical life at all and in certain monasteries in the West, in the Middle Ages, members of the clergy who were not monks took care of the monastic congregation, which was accessible to lay people. The monk, in principle, need not be a priest, although he can become it by ordination. His essential characteristic is that he does not have an "office" or function, but a special form of life which consists in not living in and for the world, but living the perfect evangelical life, which means to leave the world. It is the "heroic" life of total personal consecration to God and to saintliness. It has led as well to abandonment of the world as to great endeavours to transform it, culturally and socially.

It seems therefore right, although monasticism as such has become wholly ecclesiasticized, to say that a

[1] *Op cit.*, pp. 20 ff.

great amount of lay inspiration and aspiration has been channelled through this movement. The "wandering" preachers in the Middle Ages in France; the preaching of the Mendicant Orders, which happened till the fourth Lateran Council in 1215 without episcopal consent to a great extent through lay people; the Tertiarii and Tertiariae, who lived as secular people attached to one of the great monastic Orders, under a certain discipline of life which had a monastic-ascetic tinge, are well-known examples. They exercised, especially in the 13th century, a great influence which had considerable social consequences, particularly on the urban population. The Franciscan Tertiarii have always been the most important and are active to the present day. These fraternities and other pious associations, whose members stay in their occupations, devote themselves to works of piety and charity. The "Corpus Juris Canonici" of 1917 has defined the borders within which they have to move. The monastic knight-orders which arose also in the Middle Ages are another aspect of specific lay-expression in the life of the Church.

The more revolutionary movements in the Middle Ages, issuing from a protest against a too worldly Church and a longing for a life of poverty and evangelic simplicity. the Cathars, the Waldensians, the Lollards, were carried out by the laity. They deployed a great preaching activity and urged a return to the Bible. They were stirred to reform. They were in various respects heretics and were driven still more into heresy by the intransigent resistance of the official Church, but proved the spiritual vigour and independence of the laity, hungry for an authentic Christian life. In the Middle Ages, in which as a whole the laity was the submissive, docile part of the Church, their significance was in the charismatic field, e.g. Peter Waldes, Dante, Francis of Assisi. The Reformation, like the endeavours towards it in the preceding Conciliar Movements, when Martin Luther had tolled the bell that called forth new religious awakenings, was mainly a movement of the laity; simple men and women and also men of high standing in secular life. The Reformation in England, which has in many respects such a peculiar shape, was the work of the laity. Not only in England, but as noted already in regard to the Middle Ages, the urge for reform sprang mainly from the laity. They made the claim that the affairs of the Church were their responsibility. This conviction explains why the King in his break with the Pope, declaring himself (the most exalted layman in the realm) the supreme governor of the Church, could succeed.[1]

In this whole situation there was not only spiritual but also political fire on the altar, just as in the Reformation on the Continent social and political factors mingled with purely religious. On both sides; that of the Reformation movement and of Rome. But it remains true that in this religious revolution of great magnitude, which means at the same time one of the great turning-points of Western history, the laity produced the driving power. It is one of the clearest examples of the practical significance the laity can have and often has, independent of what one may think and define about the proper "status" of the laity in the Church. Everybody knows this. Yet, everybody hardly ever realizes it. When thinking of the Reformation, names like those of Luther and Calvin and the

[1] Cf. Dr. Kathleen Bliss in *Laymen's Work*, no. 7, June 1954, pp. 13, 14.

theological controversies occupy our thinking so completely that the other elementary fact, the enormous impetus of the laity, remains obscured. Moreover, our secularized thinking makes us easily a prey to the habit of seeing affairs of Religion and Church as a matter of clergy and theologians, whereas the rôle of the laity naturally finds its explanation in the political and social sectors. This habit or turn of mind, which is natural to us people of the modern age, makes us forget that the religious, social and political were in the 16th century inextricably intertwined, to a degree hardly imaginable to us who live in an age in which Church and Religion are meticulously delegated to their special domain. They are well kept in their place.

It is particularly interesting to note that, besides the many able laymen who participated in the Reformation by publishing religious and theological books and pamphlets—many cases from countries like France, England, Holland, Germany, Switzerland, would furnish exciting material—the great reformer John Calvin has to be mentioned as one of the most conspicuous examples in Christian history of a layman who was a self-made theologian. His famous *Christianae religionis Institutio* is—it should not be forgotten—the work of a layman, and not of a theological schoolman or a member of the clergy. Calvin's career of study covered the field of humanistic studies and of jurisprudence. His "subita conversio ad docilitatem" drove him, an extraordinarily gifted, scholarly layman, into active participation in the Reformation Movement, and to private Bible study and scholarly occupation with the sources. Not until in 1535, after the publication of the *Institutes*, the impetuous adjurations of Farel frightened him into the position of undesired leadership of the very precarious Reformation in Geneva, did he become a teacher in theology and, by necessity, minister of the congregation, or (to use the ordinary rubrics) member of the Ministry or Clergy.[1]

In spite of the fact that the layman's place of responsibility in the Church and the principle of the Universal Priesthood of Believers were strong ingredients in the Reformation Movement, in respect of Continental Europe it is largely true that, after the consolidation of the Reformation in various countries, the laity receded into the background and the Ministry or Clergy, although with different motivations and in different forms, was again established as the "office" and body which represented the Church. What in the present discussions about the Church and the laity is often described by a German term, *die Pastorenkirche* (the Ministers' Church) began its career.[2]

THE ANGLO-SAXON SETTING

The picture in the Anglo-Saxon countries is, however, in many respects different. This is mainly due to the great conflict between the Free or Dissenter Churches with the "established" Church, whether Anglican or

[1] In one of his letters (see *Corpus Ref.* IX. 443) Calvin says about allegations against him that he once had been a priest, " I have never been anything else than an ordinary layman (*laicus*) as people call it." He was M.A., Lic. of Law, and made his academic studies mainly in the field of Law and the Humanities. During his M.A. preparation he followed some courses on scholastics and the Church Fathers, but briefly. Theologically was entirely a self-taught lay theologian, who astonished people by his wide and accurate knowledge of the Fathers. It is curious to note that when he was appointed a preacher in Geneva he was introduced to his " office " without laying on of hands.

[2] In the next chapter we will enter into a fuller exposition of its causes.

Presbyterian. The "Established Church" protagonists were mainly animated by the ideal of the unity of Church and Nation. The Free Churches lived by the idea of the "gathered community" in which the laity was the essential, constituent part. The main point to make, for our purpose, is that, amidst fierce conflict and tumult, this "dissenting independist" movement was again mainly the work of the laity. They became the forerunners of the modern period of Western history, and so have exercised a deep influence in the formation of modern Western society. In these circles the creative seeds and patterns of what is now called the democratic way of life have not only been born, but have yielded the prefiguration. The principle of tolerance, which notwithstanding its many misconceptions and distortions is one of the great cultural values of the modern world, the typically modern art of discussion, aiming ideally at a common deeper understanding of truth and of finding together better and more generally satisfactory ways of solving common practical problems, to mention only some, have been born in these circles. Modern democracy owes, as to its origins, as much to these Bible-centred developments in the Christian Church as to the totally different assault of the Enlightenment.

The Quaker Movement, essentially a radical laïcization of the Church, is another example of the laity's practical significance. The 17th century is also a time in which prominent lay theologians exercised great influence. Bunyan, Milton, Leibnitz, Hugo Grotius, immediately present themselves to our minds. In more than one respect Locke may be called a lay theologian. His epochal significance as a philosophical and political thinker should not obscure the fact that he tested, as a

26

loyal Christian, his theological acumen in his *Reason-
ableness of Christianity as delivered in the Scriptures*
(1695). We may classify this nowadays in our books
on Church and cultural history under Deism, but in his
day it was the contribution of a Christian layman.

A field in regard to which the great practical significance of the laity is often overlooked is the origin and
ongoing development of the so-called Modern Missionary Movement, which owes its impetus to a great
extent to the consecration and sacrificial spirit of lay
people. The "Great Awakening" in America, the
momentous Wesleyan revival in England, Pietism as
the movement of religious regeneration on the Continent of Europe, constitute the spiritual soil from
which this amazing outburst of world-embracing
apostolic zeal sprang. The institutional non-Roman
Churches in the second half of the 17th century and the
first half of the 18th century had either solidified themselves in a safe orthodoxy (Continent of Europe) or had
gone to sleep in a comfortable latitudinarianism. The
period of orthodoxy produced, in regard to the
missionary obligation of the Church, various theories
to demonstrate that this obligation had no validity for
the Church of this period, because in some way the proclamation to the peoples of the world had happened
and had been rejected. It was a layman, the German
Justinian von Weltz,[1] who tried (1663) to demolish
these fortifications. In vain. He remained a voice in
the wilderness. The great revival movements changed
the situation entirely. Another layman, Nikolaus von
Zinzendorf, who came into contact with the Moravian
Brethren, moulded this little group of laymen into a
daring and resolute band of men and women for World

[1] Cf. J. Richter: *Missionskunde*, pp. 197 ff.

Missions. The point we want to stress here is that, in the ever-increasing missionary activity, up to the present day, the laity has found in various aspects of missionary work in non-Christian countries an outlet for its gifts and participation in the missionary task of the Church in the world. In modern Missions this has always remained the case, just as in the field of Home Missions. There could be impressive instances told of simple European laymen, living in non-Christian countries, initiating congregations of Christians single-handed, out of sheer joy to witness. The Student Volunteer Movement of the 19th century is another example of this great lay-impetus. The real point, however, is that this missionary upsurge happened mainly as a result of lay *initiative*, and was only, in its deployment, gradually recognized as the natural task of the Church and then too much clericalized. In Europe. where most (not all) missionary societies recruited their missionaries from the laity, missionaries have for a long time preserved a lay aspect because in practice they were a kind of " minor clergy ", having the right of performing full ministerial services only in their mission-field, not in the Church at home.

The characteristic feature of the 19th century in regard to the significance of the laity, as manifest in the world of non-Roman Churches, is a strong expression of organized lay activity, *apart* from the ordinary functioning of the Churches. The Roman Catholic Church produced also various new lay-movement, but they were, according to the nature of the Roman Catholic Church, always operating under some kind of clerical and hierarchical supervision. Not all activity of the lay membership of the non-Roman Churches was detached from the Church, but as a rule it was. The reasons are obvious. Since Western society emancipated itself from the authoritative guidance of the Church, and entered on a new course of secularization, the process of de-churching and de-Christianizing became inevitable. The industrial revolution with its economic, political and social consequences exercised its dissolving and disturbing effects. The Church as a whole did not find the right answer and attitude to this society in turmoil and rapid change. A host of new problems and tasks presented itself, especially in the field of human relations and conditions, which in the past, when society looked so stable, were either ignored or did not exist; and if they existed, it was not at all on such a huge scale. Political life, which nearly everywhere moved in the forms of parliamentary democracy, manifested itself in quite new expressions of civic responsibility. The enormous progress of Science, in the fields of Nature and the Spirit, called forth an inquisitive, critical mind, easily ready to question in many unusual and uncomfortable ways the truth and value of Christianity and the Christian Tradition.

This new, strongly-organized, autonomous, ever expanding lay-initiative in the 19th century, in the context of such a situation, took form in the well-known bodies, the Y.M.C.A. (1844) and Y.W.C.A. Later on the World Student Christian Federation (1896) followed. They are important features in the picture of the present "Christian" world. They all betray signs of belonging to the offspring of the "Great Awakening" and the undercurrent of Revival, which marks the 18th and 19th centuries. They are primarily evangelistic and missionary in outlook. The so-called Paris Basis of the Y.M.C.A. (1855) expresses it in the very language of the great heralds of Modern Missions: "The Y.M.C.A. seeks to unite those young men, who . . . desire to associate their efforts for the extension of His (Jesus Christ's) Kingdom amongst men ". They were determinedly international and interconfessional. They did a great deal to provide Christian nurture for young people, from Christian backgrounds, in the distraught and distracting atmosphere of the modern age. They launched out in many directions of social and cultural service. The W.S.C.F. was animated by the same missionary spirit, but concentrated on one type of people all over the world, the students. It added a new point that has proved to be full of significance for the 20th century; that is to say, the ecumenical concern. " Mission(s) and Unity ", at present a sort of credal principle of the Ecumenical Movement, has been from the outset the fundamental law of the W.S.C.F.'s existence. The Y.M.C.A. has formulated its latent ecumenical turn recently in 1955 by saying that it is " an interdenominational and interconfessional fellowship within the Church Universal ".

These fertile Youth Movements were the result of lay initiative. The names of George Williams, Henri Dunant, John R. Mott, Ruth Rouse, to take a few out of many, are sufficient to indicate this. The work as it has been carried through has always been mainly in lay hands. This is also true in regard to the aggressive 19th century evangelistic campaigns. Moody and his companions were, all things considered, charismatic laymen. It cannot be too strongly stressed that these great expressions of Christian lay-vision and sense of responsibility have performed *vicariously* a task, which in principle lies within the calling of the Church, but for which the Church as a whole was in the 19th century too clumsy, too defensive and empty of real vision.

These associations have produced many able leaders, animated by a feeling of Christian responsibility for the life of State and Society. They have been the preparatory school for the expanding Ecumenical Movement, furnishing its leadership, the drive and the vision. Especially has the W.S.C.F. continued to be an ever alert laboratory of pioneer ecumenical thinking on behalf of the whole Church on earth.

It is indubitable that this assertion of the laity as a response to Christian obedience and an expression of Christian witness is one of the great substantial facts of modern Church History. If one looks for the same period to the Roman Catholic Church, the same picture emerges. The only important difference is here that the Hierarchy not only controlled these modern eruptions of lay activity, but often guided and inspired them.

In closing our observations on these great Youth Movements, it must be said that their main significance lies in their extreme usefulness for the Church. They are not striking by their contribution to the over-arching issue of our secularist age, viz. the encounter between Church and World, and how to define that. Further, the many outstanding Christian laymen and women, who in the 19th and 20th centuries have played an important rôle *as Christians* in great public issues of the day, must be remembered.

THE "LAY ISSUE"

What has been stated so far is only a series of introductory observations to what really should be said in this chapter in order to be true to its title: "Signs of the Time". The great difference between the preceding century and the present movement is that, notwithstanding the great significance of the lay-movements we have briefly reviewed, there was no discussion of what is to-day called " the lay issue ". The layman(woman), the laity as such, were not, as is the case to-day, the centre of intense interest, the object of many declarations and pronouncements about the laity's place and contribution. In this respect our present time, as to studious consideration of the meaning and function of the laity as part of the Church, has greater similarity with the stirrings amongst the laity e.g. in the 14th century about their place in the Church than with the 19th century, which saw the birth of great well-organized lay-movements. If one sees for causes, then as the main ones should be mentioned the Ecumenical Movement, the new theological interest in the Church as a central part of the Christian Faith, and the revival of biblical orientation.

In the decades before the Second World War in various Churches there are to be observed modest attempts at what was called activization or mobilization of the laity for their fuller participation in the life and service of the Church. A quite definite view of the significance of the laity, however, found vigorous expression in the book *The Function of the Church*, written by J. H. Oldham and W. A. Visser 't Hooft in preparation for the Ecumenical Conference of 1937 in Oxford. Dr. Oldham developed in this book a thesis, to which he in later years returned often, on the strategic importance of the laity of the Church for a new and fruitful relation of Church and World, which confronted the Church with the inescapable demand to undertake a quite new teaching and educational activity in order to enable its laity to demonstrate its strategic importance. In other publications he approached the same subjects from a different angle, that is to say the urgent necessity of a theology of work and of the "common life". This approach of Dr. Oldham's was quite new, because for the first time it was not the mobilization of active laymen for various purposes considered *quite apart* from the Church, simply for its effectiveness, as Dr. John R. Mott had done in his organizing of the Laymen's Missionary Movements, but a viewing of the laity as an *expression* of the Church and its calling and function in the world. The Christian News Letter, the Frontier Movement, became in England expressions of this new approach. The deep concern behind it was the serious endeavour to show as well as to *discover* in quite new ways the relevance of the Christian Faith to all fields of life and to all modern needs and perplexities. Practically, this new approach focused often on the question how to be, in a world which in fact functioned under the rule of quite different principles and aims, a Christian in the world of one's secular occupation. It had been also Dr. Oldham who through the World Missionary Conference at Jerusalem (1928) made the "Christian" world aware of the tremendous significance of "secularism" as the all-pervading and dominant character of modern life, and of its challenge to the Church. Therefore his centering, since Oxford, on the problem of the relation of Church and World was an endeavour to find ways of answering this challenge.

On the Continent of Europe different causes summoned the laity to the foreground, especially in those countries where Nazi occupation called the Church to rethink and re-express its own credentials. A dangerous depletion of the Churches of sufficient supply of their

Ministry confronted many a congregation with the question whether it could continue to function without the regular Ministry. In grappling with this question an affirmative answer was often found, including the discovery that this new experience revealed the many talents and gifts for the ministry of the Church in the widest sense, which had always in the ordinary routine of the Church remained buried. The famous chapter I Cor. 12 on the diversities of service and gifts in the Church, which had such a long time functioned as a piece of reverent but impotent reading from the pulpit, became an eye-opener, evoking the vision of a Church with new possibilities. One of the most striking examples of this emergence of the laity was the German Evangelical Church in Silesia, which formerly had 200 pastors, who however were all, except two, evacuated when Silesia became Polish. The laymen took over the care of the Church completely. The Sunday services, including preaching, the administration of the Sacraments, religious instruction for adult and young people, pastoral care in all its forms, were looked after by the laity.

In these same countries the Churches, called to face quite new situations, experienced movements of renewal, asking themselves for an account of the stewardship of their calling in the midst of a bewildered world. In considering their laity, they came to recognize the fact that it had existed mainly as frozen credits. Moreover the simple fact that many Christian laymen in occupied countries, having out of loyalty to their principles become unemployed in their secular occupations, entered in considerable numbers into the new activities for the renewal of the Church, has impelled many people to rethink the meaning of the laity.

So the War left in this respect a very precious legacy, namely to rethink and reconsider the significance and responsibility of the laity in the Church's total expression of its being and life, and of its impact on the world. In Europe, in the period just after the War, the danger was far from imaginary that this temporary, striking lay participation would be considered as a passing emergency-phenomenon, which not only could but should disappear when the Churches recovered their "normal" condition and had again their "normal" supply of the Ministry. There have been many evidences of such an attitude and of such a deafness and blindness to the Church's real nature, and to the unprecedented immensity of the calling of the Church in a world which, though full of vigour, in fact is normless and has lost all spiritual unity. Fortunately, however, the "lay issue" which emerged out of the War was not dropped, nor smothered in the inevitable tendency to aim mainly at a return to the well-functioning institutional Church. We owe this to those acts and initiatives, on which we intend to enlarge here as "Signs of the Time".

It is unavoidable that we will deal mainly with signs in the Continent of Europe and England, because it is an undeniable fact that there the questions are most sharply formulated, and the conviction is deepest that what is intended and hoped for is not restoration but reformation. This does not imply ignoring what happens in America in regard to lay participation in the task of the Church. What happens there is quantitatively speaking far greater than in Europe and Great Britain. The enthusiasm (one might say: idealism) and devotion put into it deserve genuine respect. The Women's Movements in America have for a long time occupied a big place in the life of the Churches. The thousands of simple, but also of outstanding, men and women in the work of the Sunday School as well for adults as for children, are a strong expression of lay participation. The various big denominational Men's Movements, which have developed since the War, deploy a many-sided activity. The quantity and the intensity of activity in America dwarfs all that is done in Europe and Great Britain. Yet, for our purpose of focusing on how the "lay issue" has to be defined, we cannot escape paying most attention to Europe and what happens there. Since the 19th century American Christianity has been by far the most lay-centred form of Christianity in the world. This has, however, pragmatic reasons, not theological. So the situation in America is totally different. Not only because of—contrary to Europe—the religious boom and the respectability and popularity "religion", "any religion", enjoys there, but because America in regard to the present lay movements thinks mainly in terms of mobilization and enlistment, and only here and there in terms of a new conception of the Church.[1] In America and Europe one can speak about a "renaissance of the layman". In both parts of the world he is a much-discussed figure, but in each part the presuppositions are different.

AGENCIES OF RENEWAL

There are two main causes which have contributed to the important fact that the present call for a fuller participation of the laity in the life and task of the

[1] Centres like Parishfield (Mich.) and the "Community of Faith and Life" in the University of Texas (Austin).

Church does not only manifest itself in an increasing development of what is commonly called "Layman's Work", aiming at making this bigger and better, but is penetrating to the deeper level of what we have already called a few times the "lay issue". That is to say, to find an answer to the question of the laity's being an essential part of the Church, and not primarily an insufficiently tapped reservoir of man-power. These two main causes are (1) the various attempts to embody in new Centres new possibilities of the laity's part in the verbal and active witness of the Church in modern society, and (2) the Ecumenical Movement.

1. Many of these Centres are described in a publication by the Department of the Laity, under the title: *Signs of Renewal*. It is a post-Evanston publication, and the Epilogue in the booklet rightly asks: "Is it realistic to say that the Church *is* in its laity fully in those spheres of the world (factories, shops, political parties, government agencies etc.) where the real battles of the faith are being fought to-day? Is it not rather true that laymen and laywomen become gradually absorbed by the world because they conform to the spirit. the criteria, the hopes of this world? Do not most of the Church-members live a schizophrenic life having two different sets of ethics, one for the private Sunday life and the other for their behaviour in the workaday world? Does the Christian remnant really *live* in the world to function there as the salt of the earth? Or does it not rather stand aloof from the battlefield?"[1] I would even assert that the laity, generally speaking, feels itself spiritually powerless and illiterate as to its witness in that sector, which is the very place where most of its life is spent. This is the appalling problem, hidden by

[1] p. 59.

the fact that this laity, impotent and paralysed in the most strategic region of their life, are often faithful worshippers and do all kinds of service in the ordinary run of Church life. The problem is still more appalling because the relevancy of the Church, and what she represents in the modern world, is dependent on the conversion of this impotence and paralysis into a manifestation of power and spirit.

The Epilogue, just mentioned, also rightly says that the rise of the Centres described in the booklet is a result of the initiative of people who felt these questions as burning questions. Therefore we must take a look at some of them and try to understand them as " signs ", pointing to ever new, often disturbing discoveries of what it means to be a Christian in the present world, rather than as accomplished achievements.

The rise and growth of the Evangelical Academies in Germany must be seen on the background of the desperate situation and the spiritual and moral chaos in which Germany found itself immediately after its defeat. This has determined the name of these Institutes. By this name " Academy " they reverted to the original, not the current, significance of the word. Plato's Academy was not a school or a place of learned studies but a place of meeting and of exchange of insight. It was a place where people came for open dialogue or multilogue with each other to partake in a common search for truth about God and men. So the Evangelical Academies intended to be meeting-places for a dialogue between Church and World. After the experience of the Hitler régime when all free meeting of minds was impossible, this was quite a new beginning, and it was of great importance that Christians took the initiative.

In April 1945 the decision was taken to found the first Evangelical Academy, where people of different occupations would be able to discuss with representatives of the Church their everyday problems of belief and behaviour. On September 29, 1945 it started in Bad Boll. Since that first attempt, eighteen similar Academies have been founded in West and in East Germany. In East Germany five out of the eighteen operate, under immense difficulties, but they operate nevertheless. The Academies, bound together by the Directors' Association of Evangelical Academies, have themselves defined their aim as follows:

The E.A. are places of discourse, of fundamental rethinking and of research. They serve to meet modern man in his workaday world problems; to help him to find a way in the midst of these problems in the light of the Gospel and by so doing to testify to the unity of life in the liberty of the Gospel. The word "modern man" includes convinced Christians as well as people estranged from Church and Christian Faith. All meetings are organized and held in the light of this aim. Complete freedom of expression of whatever opinion and frank witness to the Gospel are both equally essential. The work at the Centres themselves is continued in various groups outside them, in local groups and also in publications. The Academies have a joint study-centre at Bad Boll, which develops background and basic material on the many problems that arise. As the E.A. are open to people of all colours and shades of opinion and approach, they have to be independent of any political attachment. The service they want to render is to demonstrate that the Church, because it is a ministry, creates the place where all people can meet each other in mutual respect and complete freedom.

There it must become clear that all spheres of life are under the sovereign power of God, and also that all our moral and religious behaviour, which can only find full expression in obedience to God, has to happen in a context of secular reality.

The various Evangelical Academies each have their own peculiar physiognomy, and, on the basis of a mutual understanding, specialize in various directions. These Academies are new nerve-centres in the body of old German Christendom. They launch out for a new understanding of the Church, translation of its witness, and a new understanding of the world. If they understand their constantly-growing task rightly, they must increasingly become the breeding-places of a new type of alerted and alert Christians.

The well-known German Evangelical Kirchentag has a very special significance in the question of the laity. The founder and leader is the outstanding layman Dr. R. von Thadden-Trieglaff. It started in 1949 with the first Kirchentag in Hannover. It is a large-scale effort to bring together the laity of all Churches in order to develop and express a new sense of Christian responsibility for and in all the life-sectors of the world, and to educate the laity for a courageous and spiritually intelligent witness in the world. The Kirchentag movement is sustained by an ecumenical outlook, and at the same time by the conviction that by really entering into the world and its problems, finding there the real place of Christian witness, the radical change which is required in the attitude, atmosphere and behaviour of the institutional Church might possibly be prepared, which can make the Church a place of light and healing for the nations. The work of the Kirchentag is therefore not confined to one huge yearly mass-meeting.

but goes on all the time to guide people in elaborating their new understanding of the Church, their place in it as its members, and their place in the world.

There is a solid co-operation between Kirchentag and Evangelical Academies. When one compares them it might be said that the Kirchentag moves more naturally in the ecumenical sphere and is more aware of the necessity to sink its roots in the soil of the empirical Church. These emphases are by no means absent in the Evangelical Academies, but more marginal, because they join the battle of the faith with great intensity in the German spiritual and cultural scene. In both the conviction is alive that the institutional Church by its introvert spirit and preoccupation is unable to meet the situation. In both, however, another conviction is also alive: that into whatsoever tensions and misunderstandings with the institutional Churches their work may lead them, they should not swerve from their determination to *serve* that same often blind and recalcitrant Church and confront it with new demands for better serving the world. The danger is, of course, always present (not only in Germany, but in every place where those "signs of renewal" are found) to write off the empirical Church.

The Churches everywhere have to find new patterns of congregational life and new inroads into the world, and here these new pioneering Institutes and movements can be of great help. But these Institutes and movements themselves are also under the obligation to remain at the same time single-minded and flexible. "Watch and pray" is the great demand.

It would lead too far to try to characterize, even to enumerate, the centres in other European countries. Names like Männerdorf in Switzerland, "Kerk en

Wereld " in Holland, Sigtuna in Sweden, the Iona Community in Scotland, to mention only a few, are well-known. The peculiar conditions of the countries and the peculiar personalities of the responsible leaders lend, of course, a special slant to approaches, motivations and emphases. They are, however, identical in their fundamental concern how to impress upon the laity and upon the institutional Church the idea that the laity is, notwithstanding the semblance to the contrary, the spearhead of the Church in the world.

Holland needs a brief special word, for two reasons. The first is that " Kerk en Wereld ", which started after the War, became not only a stimulating centre for meeting, study and interpretation of what a truly missionary Church means in our modern world, but also the training-centre of quite a new type of worker for the Church (the name is *Wika*) with a training, non-academic, but really adapted to the often unprecedented situations in which the Church in its traditional forms of expression fails. It is a training far more relevant than the customary ministerial training. The second is that, linked to this new attempt, the Church founded a Sociological Institute, out of the conviction that in our rapidly and incessantly changing world the Church needs not only sound theology, but also a realistic self-understanding of its concrete existence. Sociological analysis and theological understanding should support each other. Everybody who is awake to the predicament of our time agrees on this point, but the real point is that the traditional Church must itself create the instruments for a well-informed self-understanding and revision of its functioning and patterns. Study and discussion alone may enlighten the mind; they do not change the situation.

2. The Ecumenical Movement, which we mentioned as the second main cause that the "renaissance of the laity" did not exhaust itself in "lay-movements", but entered more and more fully into the search for a new conception of the laity as part of the Church, has done significant work in pressing the "lay issue" on the attention of the Churches. We have still a long way to go, because the fact must not be overlooked that one of the main results is the habit of every responsible Churchman to pay lip-service to the significance of the laity. Yet more substantial things have been achieved by the help of the Ecumenical Movement. At the first Assembly of the World Council of Churches (1948, Amsterdam) the laity as a special subject appeared on the programme under a sub-Committee. In spite of this modest position, when its report was put before the Assembly, the sub-Committee's proposal to organize Conferences on the problem of the Laity under the sponsorship of the World Council of Churches in different parts of the world was accepted. This resulted in the European Lay Men's Conference, held in 1951 at Bad Boll, and the American-Canadian one at Buffalo in 1952. Neither of these Conferences have been stirring events. Their modest result was that the strategic significance of the laity for the functioning of the Church in the present-day world, and the host of unexpected problems and issues this called forth, began to prickle and exercise more minds.

The Ecumenical Institute at Bossey was even originally conceived as a conscious attempt by the then "World Council of Churches in process of formation" to strengthen and develop the lay contribution, awakened during the War, and to give it deeper bases and wider horizons. When the Ecumenical Institute defined

itself after some years as devoted to the whole problem of Church and World, its special responsibility for
the lay problem did not abate in the least. That remained a main aspect in its programme. This appeared
in the fact that the newly created Lay-Secretariat was
placed under the leadership of Dr. H. H. Walz, who
at the same time was a member of the Institute's
Staff.

The most energetic move in the World Council of
Churches in regard to this matter of the laity was the
preparation for Section VI, The Laity, the Christian in
his vocation, of the Second Assembly at Evanston
(1954), and the decision of the Assembly to create as
part of the structure of the World Council of Churches
"The Department of the Laity". The Report of the
Section is not very striking. It was hampered by the
fact that occupation and Christian vocation in it were
too much connected as a self-evident fact, and that,
therefore, the (in itself) important problem of Work
occupied nearly half of the Report, instead of the main
point being to characterize the kind of society, of economic structure, of political organization, and of human
relations in which the Christian has to move. It would
then have offered a far more disturbing picture, in
which the seeming impossibility of the inescapable
necessity of the Christian laity's vocation to acclaim
Christ's Lordship over this secularized and demonized
world would have yielded some sound, illusionless
realism. But this illusionless realism would have helped
to fathom anew the dimension of the realism of faith,
which does not *end* but *begin* with the word that what
is impossible with men is possible with God. An
adequate view of the reality of the complicated world
of to-day is perhaps for a Christian the best inducement

to probe anew the depths of Christian belief, and to understand that the lay issue is not primarily a matter of well-organized action, but of a new grasp of the Christian Faith. The more one penetrates into what is implied in the simple phrase "being a Christian in modern society", the more one realizes our inadequacy.

The best part of the Report is the opening, under the title: The Ministry of the Laity. The short remarks explaining this title contain elements of a genuine theology of the laity, and should be gratefully acknowledged as such.

Of all the voices that are raised around the laity, the call for the lay apostolate is the strongest. The Churches, rediscovering their missionary obligation and suddenly becoming aware of the hugeness of the task, turn to the laity with the argument that every Christian is *eo ipso* a witness and a missionary: to discover next that a laity which has been so long neglected and left ignorant is in its majority unable to respond to such a demand. But it is also true that in many parts of Europe new experiments of evangelization, which often show great originality, daring and inventiveness, are being tried.[1]

The most spectacular experiment has been that of the Roman Catholic worker-priests, the more so because it ended in a spectacularly distressing way by decree of the Vatican. This admirable undertaking should, however, not obscure the fact that in non-Roman circles things happen in silence, which show an equally sacrificial spirit. However, much is happening in the Roman Catholic world, in regard to the laity, which is pertinent to our subject. It is fair to say that amongst

[1] Cf. *Ecumenical Studies on Evangelism in France, India, Scotland*, edited by H. J. Hoekendijk for the World Council of Churches.

the Roman Catholic laity, especially in France, there is a call for a new status and a new opportunity to serve the Church. It has been embodied since 1930 in "Action Catholique". Pope Pius XI has shown great interest in it in his encyclical Letters. A strong current in this movement is the desire to *be* also the Church and to play a prominent rôle in the "fonction apostolique de l'Eglise", particularly in the field of "le temporel", the common life. One of the outstanding lay-spokesmen in all these efforts is Jacques Maritain. Members of the Clergy, who are heart and soul in this movement, are often theologians with strong ecumenical sympathies, like Father H. de Lubac, Y. Congar, J. Daniélou. The literature which it has produced is immense and often of the first order. The problems discussed in the Catholic World Congresses of the laity are in many respects the same as what appears in non-Roman lay movements that are genuinely concerned about their witness in the world. The ardent participants in the Movement are determined to have done with the "passive" Church. Their burning apostolic zeal presses them to be recognized as a laity in which a specific mission, a special vocation is inherent on account of their membership of the Church, and impels them occasionally, notwithstanding their loyalty to the Church, to an independence which evokes inevitable tensions with the Hierarchy.[1]

The fact that a new appraisal of the place and responsibility of the laity emerges at the same time in the Roman and non-Roman world (the Orthodox world

---

[1] Cf. Y. Congar : *Jalons pour une théologie du laïcat*, esp. Chapters II and VIII; *Laymen's Work*, no. 7, June 1954, published by the World Council of Churches, in which from p. 24 on a very useful survey of Roman Catholic literature is to be found.

included) with such great force, and largely arising from the same causes (the relentless secularization of modern life, and the resurrected missionary sense of the Church) is a justification for speaking of " signs of the time ".

Chapter 2

THE THEOLOGICAL STATUS OF
THE LAITY IN HISTORY

THE purpose of our selective survey of the practical significance of the laity in the life and career of the Church through its history was simply to rise above the style of generalities in which this significance is usually acknowledged. Such generalities, although sincerely meant, remain too much in the sphere of a toast, in which everybody present should get his share of due appreciation. It has evidently pleased God often to use laymen to bring about important events which have given a distinctive turn to the Church's life. Dr. H. H. Walz in an article on "Adult Christianity"[1] observes that it is decisive in the next decades "whether the function of the laity will be seen in its true perspective". This is perfectly true, but somehow, in spite of all the often excellently formulated new insights and a continuing stream of equally excellent advice and exhortation in regard to the laity, the institutional Churches as such are not sufficiently alerted. This has deeper historical and spiritual reasons, into which we will look now on entering the subject of the theological status of the laity in history. We will find the amazing fact that, notwithstanding the often great, even crucial significance of the laity, they have never become really *theologically* relevant in the Church's thinking about itself. Therefore, in raising to-day the lay issue in the Church, one raises at the

[1] In *Laymen's Work*, spring 1955.

same time the demand for a new ecclesiology (doctrine of the Church).

In turning now to a short historical estimate of the laity's "theological" status, in this part of our exposition we keep silent on the testimony the Bible yields to the eager student as basic material for a theology of the laity. At this point a few remarks on the name and its origin, without entering into its theological significance, can suffice, and then we will start with the second century.

The word "lay" goes back to the Greek word *laïkos*, which in its Latinized form (*laïcus*) entered a number of Western languages. It is as a thoroughly religious word that "laïcus" has become part of the great tradition of the West. It means originally: belonging to the "laos"; that is the chosen people of God, both in the Old and the New Testament. *In this light all members of the Church are "laïkoi", and only on this basis can they get other, more specific qualifications.* It is significant to note that the word "lay", with its originally purely religious meaning, shares with some other central biblical and religious terms (e.g. "calling" and "service") the fate of having become entirely secularized. In current usage "lay" means: unqualified to speak or judge in various fields of knowledge and science. So it has acquired the notion of "ignorant". In the Latin countries "laïque" has got, as a result of the conflict between the Roman Catholic Church and modern society, the meaning of "anti-clerical", "anti-religious", "neutrality of the State in regard to religious matters". Classical Greek knew also a word for "layman" which meant a private person or an ignorant uneducated one. It is the word *idiotès*, which has fallen far deeper than *laïcus*, as

49

appears in the word "idiot". We have seen that in Acts 4:13 it is used in the sense of "uneducated", "uncultured".

As early as at the end of the 1st century it becomes evident that the significance of "laos" and "laïkos" is getting a turn, different from its basic significance in the New Testament. The main reason, apart from the profane use of the word in ancient society, is the emergence of an organized, duly ordained clergy as a closed "status" over against the "laos", the people, i.e. the ordinary congregation. The Latin Fathers often use the word "plebs". The Liturgies, which as orders of worship are the work of the clergy or priesthood, use "laos" and "populus" to denote the congregation as distinguished from the officiating priest. Another name for the *whole* Church is in the New Testament: "adelphoi", the brethren. In later documents on the structure and order of the Church, one notices the same change in "the brethren" as in regard to "laos". By "the brethren" is then meant the congregation over against bishops and deacons.[1] Clement of Rome in his Letter to the Corinthians in A.D. 95 already uses the term "laïkos" as connoting those who belong to the ordinary membership.

DEVIATION FROM BIBLICAL CONCEPT OF CHURCH

Without entering into a discussion on the historical merits and necessity of this radical change from the biblical sense of the word "laos" to the ecclesiastical sense, it is indispensable to stress that this ecclesiastical

[1] Cf. Hastings' *Encyclopaedia of Religion and Ethics*, under "Laity".

development means a deviation from the biblical concept of the *whole* Church as "laos" and as "a royal priesthood". The Church in fact became a vast body of worship, instruction, piety, activity, consisting of two clearly distinguished bodies, in which the authoritative leadership reposed in the Clergy. This duality reflected a duality in Graeco-Roman society. The Graeco-Roman city-state (polis) knew two sectors of the one body of municipal administration: the "klèros" or magistrate and the "laos" or the people. "Klèros" is the word from which the term "clergy" stems. Apart from this reference to the political-social environment in the midst of which the Church grew up into a well-organized structure, the word "klèros" has also a point of attachment in the way in which the Old Testament speaks about the Levites or priests, to whom the Lord is the "allotted portion" (klèros, Num. 18:20). The "priesthood" as the central ministry in the congregation could not but develop as the highest "office". Especially because not only, quite rightly, did the Church consider Holy Communion (the Eucharist) as the true centre of Christian worship, but gradually the Church came to be regarded in the first place as the organ for providing sacramental grace as the nourishment for eternal life. This strengthened the development of the Church's structure in the direction of another duality: those who had an "office", the leaders who were the "klèros" and the administrators (in the sense of ad-minister) of the means of Grace, and the bulk of the believers, the "laos", who were the recipients of the means of Grace, and who were led. Again, not entering into any discussion of the merits, demerits, motives, or incentives of this development, we have nevertheless to point to the fact that this is a development on a different level from that of the New Testament. "Amid the diversity of ministries in the New Testament epoch there was yet no true priesthood, for Christ was the only high priest and his the consummatory and definite sacrifice ending all the sacrifices ".[1]

W. Robinson in *Completing the Reformation. The doctrine of the Priesthood of all Believers* (1955) seems to be right in saying (p. 17): "The two words klèros (clergy) and laos (laity) appear in the New Testament, but, strange to say, they denote the same people, not different people". In corroboration he quotes Bishop J. B. Lightfoot, who wrote 80 years ago: "The only priests under the Gospel designated as such in the New Testament, are the saints, the members of the Christian brotherhood ".[2]   His concise formula (p. 20) "all Christians are God's laity (laos) and all are God's clergy (klèros) ", although in essence and intention right, is nevertheless misleading. In the New Testament the word "klèros" when it is used in regard to the new community in Christ is always meant as the body of men and women who share in God's gift of redemption and glory, which is their "inheritance" (klèros), because they are incorporated in the Son. There is no shimmer of an idea of a definite body, called Clergy. Just because the biblical content and intent of the concepts "laos" and "klèros" is essentially different from the meaning "laity" and "clergy" have historically acquired, it is confusing to use these terms with their very distinct connotations for biblical categories.

[1] Cf. *The Ministry in Historical Perspectives*, ed. H. Richard Niebuhr and Daniel D. Williams, p. 27.
[2] *The Christian Ministry*.

There are many indications that, notwithstanding the tendency we have just alluded to, biblical elements or reflections of them have continued to play a rôle. They are evident in the discussions that have cropped up at various times on the competence of the layman to teach, to take part in the spiritual life, although he belonged to the world (saeculum), and on what part the laity can have in the government of the Church. The Apostolic Fathers frequently emphasized that every Christian layman possesses a priesthood. In the first four centuries in many local congregations the laity exercised influence when a new bishop had to be elected. A very striking example is Augustine, who literally was forced to the episcopal seat by the congregation.[1]

Yet, the inherent tendency in the "ecclesiastical" line was irrepressible. Origen was the last charismatic and independent teacher. The bishops did not allow it any more. Canons 5 and 18 of the Council of Nicea define clearly not the society of the Church as a whole, but of the clerical order. The laity vanishes from the picture. The bishops in their Councils are collectively the organ of the Holy Spirit. As "spiritual" men, they exercise their divine, disciplinary and doctrinal authority, and in their collectivity may judge all things, and *be judged by none*.[2]

Particularly has the West, under the leadership of Rome, been very diligent in elaborating this fundamental pattern expressed in the simple but weighty words: "duo sunt genera Christianorum"; the clergy, including those who chose the monastic life, and the

---

[1] Cf. Y. Congar: *op. cit.*, passim, and also *The Ministry in Historical Perspectives*, first three chapters.

[2] *Op. cit.*, pp. 58, 59.

laity, sharply demarcated from each other. The line of demarcation was formed by "ordination". The "duo genera" (two bodies or classes) with increasing emphasis meant a superior and inferior class.

The Orthodox East has always kept a somewhat different atmosphere because, notwithstanding the same development into a clergy, occupying the place of authority and decision for the whole Church, and a submissive laity, it somehow kept in mind the Church as a sacramental unity of love. Many of the prominent Orthodox theologians have been and (especially in our time) are outstanding laymen.[1] Yet, precisely the deep awe for the mystery of the Sacrament has in the East stressed the unique position of the Clergy, called to handle the Holy Mysteries, and so investing them with a numinous character. As an unintentional consequence the laity became thereby degraded, and the opposition clergy-laity practically became synonymous with sacred-profane.[2] In the Roman Catholic Church the great distinction between the superior class of the Clergy and the inferior class of the Laity has been thoroughly elaborated in the "Corpus Juris Canonici" of the Roman Catholic Church, which has, in contradistinction to the Orthodox world, a different spirit, stressing not only the authority of the hierarchy but, above all, its jurisdictional authority. The Church is a "societas perfecta", but "inaequalis". The "status clericalis" and "laicalis" have each their rights and duties. The first has not only the right of administering the Sacraments and of teaching and

[1] The doctrine of "Sobornost", which affects the status of the laity, is such a private lay-theologian theologoumenon. We will come back to it.

[2] The laity has no access to the sanctuary behind the ikonostasia.

54

guidance but within its own structure has various kinds of dignity, honour and rank. The laity's rights are defined mainly in terms of obediently receiving the Sacraments, teaching and guidance. This, leaving aside the many charismatic outbursts of the laity in history or from time to time a protest against the principle of the whole system, has indelibly stamped the laity with the mark of passivity, and given them a status of secondary significance.

To understand and appreciate this development, one should not forget two points of great importance. In the first place, that in this way the hierarchical "ecclesiastical" trend believed it was giving a right expression to the supremacy of the "sacred" over the "secular" or "profane". In this view was also included the "status religiosus" of the monastic orders, which conceived the truly religious life, the "perfect Christian life", in terms of an (ideally speaking) complete severance from all that constitutes the ordinary "secular" or profane life. In regard to the laity, this signifies that they belong entirely to the "secular" order, to the world, with which in the perspective of the normative "perfect Christian life" one ought to break all binding ties. This implies a definite devaluation of the world and of the natural human relations, interests and occupations, and consequently a devaluation of the laity. The slow but inevitable development towards celibacy as an obligation for the clergy is not only an infiltration of the monastic idea on the "spirituality" of the secular clergy but the logical outcome of the stratification of the "lower" temporal and the "higher" or only commensurate spiritual order. It is again on this point that the Eastern Orthodox world has maintained a less logical and less rigid attitude.

"WESTERN" AND "EASTERN" DEVIATION

Looking at this whole development, which led theoretically and practically to the devaluation of the laity as to its place and responsibility in the Church, and to the extolment of hierarchical power and authority, the Western and the Eastern Church were in fact unbiblical, though certainly not in intention. From the historical point of view this process becomes in many respects very understandable. The suggestions radiating from the social and political patterns of the world in which the Church grew up and had to build its own structural organizations, the inner and outer dangers asking for effective and strong leadership and authority against dilution and dissolution, pushed the Church rather in the direction of a body of doctrine and authority than of nearness to the biblical pattern of the new, transformed community, in which the diverse gifts and ministries manifested the supreme source of life and direction in the Church: the Holy Spirit.

A very clear example of stressing this "ecclesiastical" line of development under the pressure of historical forces, while at the same time in intention sincerely wanting to be biblical, is Irenaeus.[1] He says in one of his writings: "all the righteous possess the sacerdotal rank"; "all the disciples of the Lord are Levites and priests". This is certainly not devaluation of the laity. It purely reflects the biblical perspective. Yet Irenaeus was, in the great struggle of his days, one of the architects of the "ecclesiastical" development. We are worlds apart from this sensitive equilibrium of

[1] Cf. article on "Laity" in Hastings, op. cit.

deep "biblical" awareness and of being an instrument in a historical interplay of forces impelling towards "ecclesiastical" structure, in the famous Bull "Unam Sanctam" of 1302 issued by Pope Boniface VIII. Some words of the Gospel are simply used here to motivate and justify the *power* of the spiritual order (represented by the successor of Peter) above that of the temporal order. The total biblical teaching about the Church and about her relation to the world, which is so rich and varied and surprisingly new, is reduced here to a simplistic interpretation of the story of the two swords in Luke 22:38, and to a matter of absolute power of the Church and of delegated power to the existing authorities of the world. C. W. Mönnich[1] rightly observes that the most astonishing thing in the Bull is not so much the abuse of biblical words, but rather the fact that the decisive motivation for this "power"-construction is the Neo-Platonic philosophy of Dionysios the Areopagite about the cosmic gradation of spheres from the divine being to matter.

The importance of the quotation from Dionysios the Areopagite in "Unam Sanctam" is that thereby is revealed to us the real reason for the development of the Church which led to a devaluation of the world, or the secular, and of the laity. It is that, both in doctrinal and in structural respect, a development which was inevitably embedded in historical relativities and contingencies was absolutized and given a sort of suprahistorical metaphysical status, founded in the given structure of the cosmos. Nothing is more alien to the whole spirit and tendency of the Bible than just this kind of philosophical thinking.

Behind this great distinction between "temporal"

[1] In *Laymen's Work*, June 1954, p. 9.

or "secular" order and "spiritual" order lies a conception kindred to the duality which occurs in all the religions of the world. The great French sociologist E. Durkheim has expressed it in his famous book *Les formes élémentaires de la vie religieuse* in the formula that the fundamental distinction in all religions is that between "profane" and "sacré". We will come back to the point that the historical-empirical Church, since both in East and West the "ecclesiastical" line of thinking got the upper hand over the "biblical" one, has too easily brought the relation "Church" and "World" under the universal religious distinction of "sacred" and "secular". Since Ignatius and Cyprian had stated clearly "the Church is constituted by the bishop and his clergy", the "ecclesiastical-hierarchical" type of thinking became more and more dominant. The laity so to speak were taken for granted. And since[1] the monastic conception of a life of special saintliness began to influence the way in which the special quality of life, the "spirituality", of the clergy had to be conceived, the laity inevitably fell into a lesser category of saintliness. Their life-condition afforded them lesser possibility of a saintly life. It is inherent in this strongly hierarchically conceived idea of the Church and in this identification of "holy" or "saintly" (in the sense of "perfect") with "sacral" that, if there is an endeavour to define the laity, it can be done only negatively, viz. by distinction from the clergy. They are in the world and do not belong to the world of the "sacred" or "sacral", the special domain of the clergy. The present-day discussions about the laity in the Ecumenical Movement are still suffering from this same inhibition.

[1] Congar, *op. cit.*, expounds this very clearly.

Gratian in the 12th century gives on this background a clear description of the two "kinds" (genera) of Christians, the two "peoples" (populi) in the Church. There is one "genus", devoted to the divine office and to contemplation and prayer, thereby diverted from all occupation with temporal things. This "genus" is the Clergy. They are kings (reges), that is to say by their virtues and therefore in God ("ita in Deo") they rule themselves and others. There is another kind of Christian, viz. the laity. They are permitted to possess temporal goods, but only for their own use. In the nature of a concession they are permitted to marry, to cultivate the soil, to exercise jurisdiction between man and man etc. and "can find salvation if they have avoided vice by doing good".[1] Gratian leaves no doubt that the condition of the laity is an unavoidable concession to human frailty. Life in the world and devoted to the interests of the world is *eo ipso* a compromise, precisely because retirement from the world guarantees a life without compromise; in other words, the authentic Christian life.

In spite of its impressive logic, favoured moreover by the feudal sense of life and man in the Middle Ages, this conception of the Church and its two "kinds" of Christian never reigned supreme. In the struggle between the Pope and the Christian kings and emperors, there were voices raised not only in favour of a less dependent or even an independent position of the "temporal" powers from the "spiritual" power embodied in the Pope; but this implied a far more positive appreciation of the secular and, consequently, of the place of the laity and of the nature of the Church. It sounds like an antiphon to Ignatius': "The Church

[1] Cf. Congar, *loc. cit.*, p. 27, note 21, and p. 30, note 26.

consists of the bishop and his clergy ", when Philip IV, king of France, in his controversy with Boniface VIII says: "Ecclesia non solum est ex clericis, sed etiam ex laïcis ".[1]

One outstanding example is Marsilius Paduensis, who in his *Defensor Pacis* went back to biblical and patristic data and conceived of the Church as the "Societas fidelium", in which both clergy and laity had their well-defined place and voice. The hierarchical conception of the Church was under attack. Dante did it out of prophetic indignation in his *Divine Comedy*; men like Marsilius were inspired by revolutionary political ideas, which were an early but very outspoken prelude on the coming democratic future. The conciliar movement of the 14th and 15th centuries, although meant as a reformation in head and members of the Church, reflected the rising nationalism and independent sovereignty of the different States against the papal claim of authority over both Church and State more than it represented a downright attack on the hierarchical structure of the Church. But in all these vigorous protests and movements a greater appreciation of the place of the laity was also implied.

The relevance of the laity received the greatest emphasis in the sectarian apostolic movements after the 12th century, and especially in the 14th century through Wiclif. The specific significance of this peculiar set of protests and movements is that their inspiration was purely religious. They squarely confronted the "ecclesiastical-hierarchical" line with the "biblical" one. They were of course not wholly unaffected by repercussions of the conflict between the

[1] "The Church consists not only of the clergy but also of the laity." Congar, *op. cit.*, p. 61, note 28.

worldly-conceived papal theocracy and the nationalistic demands of the nations and their rulers for an independent status, but their heart lay really with a reform of the Church in the light of the Word of God.[1]

RADICAL CHANGES INAUGURATED BY THE REFORMATION

The fundamental ideas of the Reformation promised to inaugurate a radical change in the whole conception and place of the laity. Luther, at a decisive moment, rejected obedience to the Church as embodied in the hierarchical authority of the Pope, in the name of obedience to the Word of God. Luther's conception of the Church, especially in his earlier, militant writings, was a frontal attack on the hierarchical conception of the Church. The idea of the clergy as such was rejected. In principle the distinction of "clergy" and "laity" fell away. In his manifesto *To the Christian Nobility* he proclaimed: "All Christians are truly priests and there is no distinction amongst them except as to office. . . . Everybody who is baptized, may maintain that he has been consecrated as a priest, bishop or pope". For the sake of order alone certain

[1] Looking back on these struggles, one is again and again struck by the daring and the independence of mind shown in the Middle Ages, a time which is always considered to be marked by submissiveness, especially to authority claimed on religious grounds as necessary to salvation. This amazement increases when one takes into consideration our own time, which regards itself by definition as *the* time of non-submissiveness. Nevertheless whatever movements of protest and conflict there may be in the Roman Catholic world of to-day against the hierarchy, they are very weak in daring and independence in comparison with those of the Middle Ages. In our secularistic age, in which submissiveness is devaluated on principle, the submissiveness to the hierarchical claims of the Church has never before been so undisputed.

people are set apart by the congregation, "ministers" who were not priests in the cultural sense, mediators between God and the congregation or God and man, but "ministers of the Word" (*verbi divini ministri*). But in principle all that was contained in the newly conceived ministry (to teach and preach, to baptize, to administer Holy Communion, to bind and loose sins, to make intercession, to judge about doctrine and discern the spirits) belonged of right to every baptized Christian. This meant the universal priesthood of the believers or, as is often said, the priesthood of all believers, which has since, coupled with the rule of *sola gratia, sola scriptura*, been proclaimed as the great formal principle of the Reformation and of Protestantism in particular.

In these militant propositions there is a germ of individualism, of equalitarianism, which does not sound wholly consonant with the biblical view of the "royal priesthood" which belongs to the body of Christian believers as a whole.[1] This militancy and this extravagance of expression is understandable in view of the fact that Luther had to fight a formidable system of hierarchical thinking, deeply entrenched in the minds of men, borne by the prestige of ages, and had to call it to account before the forum of the biblical idea of the Church and its membership. His attack, fully justified, implied the abolition of all clericalism, and the most emphatic vindication or rehabilitation of the laity ever uttered.

And yet it must be frankly stated that neither this new conception of the Church nor this strong vindica-

[1] T. F. Torrance, *Royal Priesthood*, p. 35, note 1, criticizes in this light the expression "priesthood of all believers" as an unfortunate one "as it carries with it a ruinous individualism".

tion of the laity has ever become dominant. The much-vaunted principle of the "priesthood of all believers" had certain consequences of great interest in the New World, but as a rule in the Old World it never became really efficacious. To the present day it rather fulfils the rôle of a flag than of an energizing, vital principle. Undoubtedly through the Reformation and the variety of Churches which issued from it, the "ecclesiastical-hierarchical" line of conceiving the Church will never regain the undisputed position it had before. The call to justify any doctrine of the Church and the function of its membership before the tribunal of biblical evidence will never again be so ignored as before. Calvinism's ethical orientation of its lay members towards demonstrating the reality of their state of election by a wholehearted management of their work has been a consequence of the doctrine of "the universal priesthood of the believers" which had world-historical consequences. Still, it cannot be denied that this doctrine or principle has, especially in the 19th century under the influence of liberalistic-individualistic thinking, become more a theme of theological declamation in order to recommend the Protestant variety to the modern mind than a spiritual, Church-transforming power.

Why did Luther's and Calvin's new definition of the Church, the Ministry and the central and primary place of the congregation as a whole remain in the long run a declaration of principle rather than become increasingly a fact? Why did the Ministers become dominant instead of the congregation (*die Gemeinde*) as a whole?

We will mention first some fundamental reasons, irrespective of the historical circumstances, which have exercised a great influence. The Reformers, in returning to the Bible and finding there that the Lord Jesus Christ is the only true Head of the Church, ruling the whole Church by His Holy Spirit and by His grace and forgiveness, eliminating all gradation of powers, rights and authority, were determined to have done with the system of hierarchical gradation, and the identification of the Church with the priestly-sacramental clergy. The Church was a body of believers and forgiven sinners. But in organizing or reorganizing the Church their attention was mainly turned to the avoidance and elimination of the flagrant abuses and corruptions of the dominant system. The Reformers' thinking on the Church did not become fully biblical, because quite understandably in the stress and heat of the battle it was strongly determined by protest and polemics. Moreover, Luther's defiant words that every baptized Christian had the power which the Pope, bishops and priests have, hid some pitfalls.

In the first place, this one: that in a centuries-old Church "baptized Christian" is far from synonymous with a truly believing Christian. Therefore, though it was rightly assumed that the directive power and authority for the conception and ordering of the Church resided in the biblical pattern of the Church, it did not necessarily follow that this pattern had to be imitated. For different historical situations demand different creative expressions of the same fundamental directives. In the second place, the former members of a Church which for ages had kept its membership in a state of spiritual immaturity, concealed by the doctrine of "implicit faith" of the laity, could not suddenly function as spiritual adults.

In the third place, the Reformation coupled with its radical elimination of the distinction between "clergy" and "laity" a vehement stress on the pre-eminence of the preaching office (*die reine Predigt*). This vehement stress on correct, "pure"[1] *preaching* as the sustaining nourishment, required (leaving aside other considerations) a specially qualified group of bearers of this office (*Amt*). The right administration of the Sacraments, which was also emphatically proclaimed as one of the essential marks of the Church, did not, however, in many Churches, particularly in regard to the Eucharist, obtain the same position as the "pure preaching of the Word". Its administration was reserved for the "ministry". Although this development had many good reasons, it kept an inner ambiguity in the whole conception of the "ministry", because on the one hand it tended towards a re-establishment of a kind of "clergy", whereas on the other hand the abolition of the distinction between "clergy" and "laity" was, at least in principle, maintained. Ordination to the status of *rite vocatus*, which had become the wall of separation between "clergy" and "laity" in the early Church, became in fact again a sort of dividing line. As already observed, it was motivated by the argument that this distinction happened for the sake of order. In the light of the principle of "the universal priesthood of believers" and what was meant by it, this is of course the only right motivation. It wanted to express, in answer to the priestly-sacramental conception of the past, a definite adieu to the idea of the indelible character of the "clergy" as existing in elevated isolation from the laity. Yet, in fact, contrary to the theory of funda-

[1] i.e. adequate interpretation of the Word of God.

mental non-distinction, it encouraged the practical recognition of a secondary status of the "laity" in comparison with the ministry, the breeding of an attitude of passivity in the laity as a whole, the accentuation of the significance of "office" (*das Amt*) and its leadership.

This trend of development was strengthened by the fact that the ministers, whose main work was considered to be the right preaching of the Word, appeared more and more as the "theologians", the "knowers", and in the existing framework of social stratification and honour they represented the "spiritual status" (*geistlicher Stand*); in other words the *pneumatikoi*, the *spiritual persons* (1 Cor. 3) by profession. Its counter-effect was that the laity gradually got into and, generally speaking, accepted the position of the "ignorant", the spiritually non-adult. It has led to the situation, which is at present still prominent, that there is in all Churches a clear division between the leading office-bearers and the laity, functioning on the tacitly accepted assumption that, properly speaking, the Church is essentially the concern of the ministry. Already at the time of the Reformation and in the first period of its consolidation, concrete historical facts ensured that the principle of "the universal priesthood of believers" could not be acted upon. The Reformers originally did not intend to establish a new Church. What interested them in the first place was the purification of the faith. When, however, the stubborn resistance of the leadership of the Church drove them to organize Church life on the basis of their own principles, they were speedily confronted by the problem of the ignorance of the laity and the difficulty of establishing decent order in the congregations. This was the case not only in Germany but in England, where the Reformation was less drastic and systematic.[1]

Besides, the actual organizational Reformation could not be carried out without the help and authority of princes and political magistrates who were in favour of the Reformation. This resulted gradually in the princes and political magistrates occupying a great place in Church matters. The laity, even when not ignorant, saw no other possibility than leaving matters in the hands of the ministers and the state bodies created for administering Church life. As early as 1526 Luther confessed that for his ideal of a true Christian congregation he had not yet available a sufficient number of Christian people and he did not even see many who insisted that it should be undertaken. The organization that developed did not give a status to congregations which provided for active responsibility. They were objects of ministerial and pastoral labours and governmental regulation. Consequently the laity, although in a setting different from that before the Reformation, remained as of old, *objects*, and in no sense became *subjects*. Calvin, who in distinction from Luther had to grapple with the same problem in one city and not in different *Länder*, succeeded better in his "Ordonnance ecclésiastique" of 1541 in realizing a relative independence of Church life, which was also due to his very distinct idea of the divinely instituted polity of the Church. It was the most dynamic of Church orders which issued from the Reformation. His high conception of the excellence, indispensability and authority of the minister, necessitated by the need for a well-led Church, implied

[1] I owe very much to W. Pauck's contribution in *The Ministry in Historical Perspectives*, pp. 110-147, for the following observations.

however involuntarily a neglect of the real significance and relevance of the laity.

The New World quite naturally shows some special features.[1] The history of America is a long series of adaptations and readaptations to a new world with new conditions and a constant shift of changes. Originally the Church in America was a European Church, transplanted into a quite new environment. In the process America developed a new type. Ever new immigrations, and especially the great waves of immigration in the 19th century, kept this process going. The result has been that parochial and self-governed Churches are distinctively American, which has made for greater control and participation of the laity. Under the aegis of the deeply-cherished principles of religious liberty and the separation of Church and State, the Church has become conceived as the voluntary association of the saved and as an institution for improving public life by saving individuals. Urbanization has forced the Churches to reach out to all kinds of people and groups, and has favoured the tendency of American Churches to strengthen the inner fellowship of the local Church. The lay ministry in various forms has greatly grown as a result of these developments.

In comparing European and American Church life, one is tempted to say that the inherited structure and mood of European Churches is, generally speaking, not greatly encouraging to lay initiative. In America the reverse is true. It is not any theoretical reasoning about the responsibility of the laity which brings this about in America, but the pragmatic consideration that the usefulness of the Church as an effective institution

[1] Cf. *op. cit.*, pp. 207 ff.

depends almost entirely on the willingness of the laity to commit themselves.

In closing this selective historical survey of the theological status of the laity, we want to make a few more remarks. In the 19th century, at the time when the wave of unchurching and dechristianization began to show its vigour, Johann Heinrich Wichern,[1] the Father of the "Innere Mission" in Germany, tried to actualize the Reformation "principles" of the universal priesthood of believers. He interpreted it, not in the usual way as "having direct intercourse to God" without any priestly mediation, but as an obligation to "diakonia", valid for the whole membership of the Church. The dynamism of the "communio sanctorum" lies in the fact, he said, that it is not only the "congregatio vere credentium" (the assembly of the true believers) but most certainly the "congregatio vere amantium" (the assembly of the true lovers). This points already in a new direction.

WOMEN—FULLY PART OF THE LAITY

There is one aspect of the lay issue which needs special mention, viz. the place and responsibility of women in the Church. In this little book it is axiomatically assumed that in the word laity men and women are equally included. The women members of the Church are as fully part of the "laos" as the men members. There is, however, no subject on which the Christian Church has always been (and in most cases still is) so retrograde, so subject to non-Christian, pagan notions of the sexes and to patriarchal thinking as in regard to women and their place in the Church.

[1] Cf. Martin Gerhardt: *J. H. Wichern.* Hamburg, 1927.

Nobody denies the great significance and contribution to the life of the Church on the part of women. This does not, however, alter the fact that, generally speaking, the place and rights of women in the Church are treated on the basis of non-Christian and sub-Christian ideas. It is striking that in recent years in many Churches in the world the question of the place and rights of women has been debated with great force. The recognition of the equality of women with men in society, economic and political life, and the growing realization of this recognition shows up the inferior position of women in the Church more and more as an unbearable anomaly. The inferior position of women (in the sense of an inferiority inherent in their sex, i.e. in nature) is, however, not only a cultural lag, still dragging on in the Church, but is chiefly so deeply rooted in the Churches because it depends on the question of what should be considered the right interpretation of the Scriptures. This puts the whole dispute on the status and rights of women and of their inherent inferiority on a different level. Not on the level of nature, but on that of God's ordering of nature and of obedience or disobedience to the Word of God.

The fierce debate, fiercer than ever before in history, on the rightful place of women in the Church is thus inextricably intertwined with the still undecided inner debate within the Church about the interpretation of Scripture, either according to the line of the letter that killeth or according to that of the spirit that vivifies. Behind these debates about disobedience or obedience to the divine Word there are, of course, hiding themselves also all the sociological and psychological inhibitions which together build up the deeply entrenched masculine superiority assumption. This still prevailing lack of decision in regard to the right scriptural interpretation, and the general conservative temper in the Church as to the status of women, are common to ministry and laity (many women included). It is, therefore, of the greatest importance that this woman question is seen as a part of the whole problem of the place of the laity in the Church, i.e. both men and women, as the " new creature in Christ ". From that angle all questions and arguments about superiority-inferiority automatically fall out, however differently men and women are " placed " as to functions and possibilities, as being in that context irrelevant.

"THE LAITY MAKE THE CHURCH"

In our survey we saw how extremely little the place of the laity was developed in the thinking of the Church between the 2nd and the 16th centuries along what we called the " hierarchical-ecclesiastical " line. It is truly amazing to find at present in the Roman Catholic Church, which in its Canon Law regards the Church mainly as an organization of the sacramental cultus, the most vigorous expressions on the place of the laity as an essential part of the Church. The latest publication of the " Corpus Juris Canonici " was in 1917, before the pressure of the secularized world called forth in the Roman Catholic Church a new apostolic awareness. This new apostolic zeal expressed itself in the " Action Catholique ", a great movement of the lay apostolate. Various Popes were fully awake to the great significance of this apostolic eagerness of the laity and took care to keep it under the supervisory direction of the Church, and at the same time to stimulate and guide it in their allocutions and encyclicals. Pius XII has not hesitated, strange as it may seem in a Church so supremely "clerical" in its core, to express this new, never-foreseen importance of the laity for the Church's battle in the world in the terse words: "The laity are the Church; they make the Church." These words do not of course mean a radical laïcization of the Church, although they *could* serve as a motto for such an undertaking. Nothing else, however, could better indicate the crucial importance of the lay issue for all Churches in the world than these words in the mouth of the Pope. It is high time that the leadership of other Churches showed the same clear-sightedness and determinate action. Congar has rightly grasped the opportunity to design in this "large contexte de renouveau ecclésiologique "[1] a theology of the laity.

The general conclusion that can be drawn at the end of this chapter is that for the greater part of its history the Church has provided little place in its thinking for expressing the meaning of the laity in the divine economy of salvation of the world and in the economy of the Church. At best the laity was the flock; always it was object, never subject in its own calling and responsibility. When, as with the Reformation, in principle a strong vindication of the laity as *subject* and not merely *object* was made, the plea in concrete reality broke down on the general inaptitude of the laity to function as a subject in the biblical sense, and (even partly as a consequence of this sordid reality) on the enormous preoccupation with the raising and implementing of the ministry. This ministry though not in theological theory, yet certainly in the realities of sociological structure and psychological apprehen-

[1] "Broad context of ecclesiological renewal." *Op. cit.*, p. 9.

sion, became in many respects a metamorphosis of the former "clergy". The priestly-sacramental notions related to the "clergy" were of course largely eliminated and re-interpreted in a religious-moral sense; but in actual fact the "standing" and "apartness" of the new-born "ministry" were in many respects similar to those of the former "clergy".[1]

In our time again, the Church is more emphatically than ever before called to give account of the meaning of the laity for the Church and the World. Therefore every serious attempt to participate in this accounting can be significant.

[1] In saying this I am not forgetful of the fact that some of the Free or Dissenting Churches (Baptist, Methodist etc.) gave and give prominence to the laity, in theory and practice; but we will look at that later on.

Chapter 3

IS A THEOLOGY OF THE LAITY
POSSIBLE?

AFTER this attentive glance at the practical
significance of the laity and of its theoretical status
in the various great confessional types, it seems
as if the stage is now set for designing a theology of
the laity. This would, however, be too rash a conclusion, for the simple reason that to try one's hand at
such an attempt implies a reorientation of all existing
ecclesiologies (doctrines of the understanding of the
Church). Even more, it presupposes a new *total*
ecclesiology. Congar states it quite clearly: " Au
fond, il n'y aurait qu'une théologie du laïcat valable:
une ecclésiologie totale ".[1] Other people than Congar
have expressed this conviction, but, notwithstanding
the liveliness and intensity of the present discussion on
the lay issue, it is doubtful whether the implications
of such a vigorous dictum are seen with sufficient
realism.

The ecumenical discussions of the last decades
prove that the hard core in this discussion is just:
ecclesiology, the different doctrines on the structure of
the Church, the "ministry" and the conditions of its
validity, the Sacraments and their valid administration.
The ecclesiologies of the different Churches (with the
exception of some which have come into being by a
conscious taking into account of the idea of "the

[1] " Fundamentally, there is but one valid theology of the laity;
that is to say, a whole ecclesiology." *Op. cit.*, p. 13.

universal priesthood of believers") are as a rule in their fundamental emphases and stresses conceived in such a way that a real theology of the laity would hardly find a place in them.

The host of writings that have sprung up around the revived interest in the place and significance of the laity in the Church and in the world contain already many *ébauches*, many first rough sketches of a theology of the laity, also full of suggestions in regard to a change of structure of the Church in the face of the totally-changed structure and character of our society. The numerous experiments towards new forms of real Christian fellowship and being the Church in unorthodox ways (house-churches, occupational congregations, para-parochial congregations) are heartening, and demonstrate at the same time that a theology of the laity affects not only the doctrine of the Church in its totality, but also its structure. Both, "une ecclésiologie totale" and the structure of the Church, which are implied in the existing ecclesiologies, are in the balance when a theology of the laity is proposed. Not as an interesting and even inspiring piece of new theological thinking, but as a serious attempt at *reform* of the Church.

A NEW SPRINGTIME OF THE CHURCH

Many of the already published *ébauches* of a theology of the Church are indeed of great value. They suggest, taking their inspiration from renewed Bible study, approaches to a new self-understanding of the Church, which contains essential points. They are visionary and dynamic, and therefore cause for great gratitude. In the nature of the case, being first attempts, they are eye-openers and way-openers, and as such augur much good. If they remain however in the long run only visionary and dynamic, and do not achieve a radical reorientation of the existing and still obtaining ecclesiologies, then " a theology of the laity " would, as to its effect, at its best mean a welcome injection into the hardened veins of the existing Churches, or a welcome appendix to the official thinking on the Church.

This certainly would be of no little value. Indeed, it would be a great thing. It would, however, underestimate the enormous power of historic moulds of thinking, principles, attitudes, and institutions, which naturally tend to an inertia which prevents a rejuvenation in head and members.[1] For it should constantly be kept in mind that the driving force behind all the present endeavours, in theory and in practice, to find and express the true place and significance of the laity for the manifestation of the Church's nature and calling, is the prayerful hope and longing for *a renewal of the Church*, or as Congar says a " nouveau printemps de l'Eglise " (new springtime of the Church).

On the basis of these considerations it seems commendable to devote some space to the implications of the vigorous dictum that a " theology of the laity " in fact means a reorientation of ecclesiology as a whole (" une ecclésiologie totale "). A striking example of the difficulties inherent in this dictum is Congar's substantial volume on a theology of the laity. This book is not only a storehouse of very precious information

[1] The recent commotion in Sweden about the decision of the Synod not to permit women entrance into the ministry, shows a remarkable antithesis between " clerical " and " lay " thinking. This antithesis is one of the latent facts in many Churches all over the world and is too much ignored. It should be dispassionately analysed as to its real causes.

76

on a great variety of subjects, but it demonstrates visibly the fascinating contest between the demands and consequences of a new dynamic approach and a Church which is a model of historic continuity and, therefore, of historic tenacity. We will take therefore a rather long look at it.

Congar begins by contrasting two things. One is the renewal of the Church in its various aspects, and the impetus behind it, expressed in the words: "the laity belongs fully to the Church"; one of the mottoes of the "Congrès mondial de l'Apostolat des Laïcs" in 1951 at Rome. The other is that the "Corpus Juris Canonici" of 1917 has no place of any significance for the laity. It codifies the rights of the clergy, because the clergy *is* the Church as being eminently a sacramental body. It reflects the mediaeval distinction of the "sacerdotal" and the "temporal". The laity are envisaged under the angle of the "temporal" and of their submission in the "spiritual". The subordination of the laity to the hierarchy and their receptive, passive position is the expressed and unexpressed presupposition.

In our modern world there is, says Congar, an imperative need for a militant Christian life. This necessitates a theology of the laity, which by the magnitude of the problems cannot but mean a total revision of the ecclesiology of the "Corpus Juris Canonici". He especially stresses the point that such a theology of the laity cannot simply be an appendix of an "ecclésiologie-cléricale"![1] Congar shows his clear-sighted determination also in his announcement of a still forthcoming publication, e.g. on the principle of Consent: "quod omnes tangit ab omnibus tractari et approbari debet" (what affects everybody should be

[1] p. 13.

discussed and approved by everybody). The real difficulty implied in this daring programme becomes, however, immediately apparent when he goes on to say[1]
that, just as in his studies on Ecumenism and on Reform
in the Church, his guiding principle will be that of
developing this theology of the laity along the line
of a doctrine of the *life* of the Church, developing itself
within the framework of the *structure* of the Church.

Later on[2] he becomes more explicit on this crucial
point. He speaks then about the Church having two
aspects: 1. The Church, in its ultimate reality, is the
community of men with God and with each other, in
Christ (*Societas fidelium*). 2. The Church is also the
sum-total of means of this community (the hierarchy
and its authority, the magisterium of the Church, its
priesthood, its *potestas*, its sacraments). This dual doctrine is in Congar's view the doctrine of the New
Testament, the Apostolic Fathers and Tradition. In
many other places he uses the terms "principe communautaire" and "principe hiérarchique"[3] and maintains that the hierarchical structure and principle
is what is given by Christ and which produces the
communal principle. The hierarchical structure or
institution is of the two aspects the primary one,
as well ontologically as in regard to order. The
"corps ministériel hiérarchique" is the real representative of Christ. The Church as Hierarchy precedes
"ontologiquement" the existence of a Community,
for the Church has been a Church of priests before
it was a Church of believers. The Church as priestly
Hierarchy is more than the "pure communauté des
fidèles", because life is fluid and changing, structure is

[1] p. 16.   [2] p. 48.
[3] This is of course in the Roman Catholic sense.

78

stable and unchanging. He recognizes frankly that the Roman Catholic Church has always shown a strong tendency to stress the hierarchical principle in a very unilateral way and that the present insistence of the laity to be accepted fully as a real part of the Church is a revolt against this clericalism. Yet, in keeping the two aspects simply together and in pleading for the rights of the "principe communautaire" without entertaining any critical reconsideration of the "principe hiérarchique" in its concrete Roman Catholic embodiment, Congar's magnificent book fails in its claim to develop a theology of the laity which is not an appendix to an "ecclésiologie cléricale", but an integral part of a total ecclesiology, which he often expresses in the word "ecclésiale" over against "ecclésiastique".

It is obvious to say that one could hardly expect anything else from a Roman Catholic theologian, even one with such a prophetic and missionary temperament as Congar, than to regard the doctrine of the Church as sacrosanct. That is true, but the result is that in such a case a theology of the laity cannot but become an appendix and a number of corrections on a too one-sided hierarchical structure. It cannot become an integral part of the theological self-understanding of the Church. It will have a certain vogue as long as a certain situation makes it useful and helpful. The strong utterances in the Papal Encyclicals about the extreme importance of the laity, honestly meant as they are, do not, when one reads them attentively, make the impression that they are the building-material for a fully developed theology of the laity, long neglected but at last adopted. They have more the ring that the laity are at present exceedingly important, even more so than the clergy, because on them the efficacy of the Church in the present secularized world depends. Which is quite true.

A Church such as the Roman Catholic Church, which proclaims that it is *jure divino* a hierarchical Church, embodying continuity and infallibility, can only have a marginal interest in a real theology of the laity. But this cannot be said of Congar's book. He develops as far as his self-imposed limits allow him an impressive wealth of ideas and suggestions to help the laity feel themselves a real part of the Church and its task in the world. The theme is evidently one of passionate concern to him. His basis is the famous 16th century doctrine of the three messianic offices (*munera*) of Christ: the royal, the priestly, the prophetic of which he gives an excellent biblical sketch. The Church as His representative has the same offices, which find their reflection in her acts through the behaviour and duties of her members, making them not only objects, but real subjects.

RE-THINKING THE SYSTEM

We have put as title to this chapter the question: Is a theology of the laity possible? Meaning thereby: is it possible as an integral, not as an additional, part of the total self-understanding of the Church, and claiming that, if it is meant as an integral part, it necessitates a rethinking of the existing doctrines of the Church. The example treated in Congar's book has yielded the conclusion that the refusal to undertake such a rethinking of the system itself (however understandable the refusal may be in this case) results in a theology of the laity, which is an amendment to something which is *eo ipso* unalterable. The attempt to infuse new elements and energies into the unalterable doctrine by means of the more dynamic doctrine of the royal, priestly and prophetic offices of the Church as a whole, opens up many possibilities of greater flexibility, but as soon as e.g. the question of the laity's voice and authority in the Church as a whole is raised,[1] the finger of exclusive priestly voice and authority is immediately raised also. In turning now to the non-Roman ecclesiologies, we certainly do not encounter that spirit of rigid authoritarian unalterability which characterizes the Roman Catholic doctrine. Nevertheless, it is worthwhile to look into the matter with the question in mind whether within the spirit and frame of the non-Roman ecclesiologies a theology of the laity fits in naturally, as an integral part, not as a useful appendix.

One's anticipation is to be inclined to an affirmative answer, especially when thinking about the various ecclesiologies which sprang from the Reformation, which was so strongly animated by revolt against the rigid priestly authoritarianism of the Roman Catholic Church. On closer investigation there arises some doubt, which is partly suggested by the fact that, in spite of the sincere and forceful proclamation of the "universal priesthood of believers" and even of the place and authority in various Church orders accorded to lay people, the laity as such has remained a passive element. It is also suggested by some other peculiarities, which pass in the main unnoticed. In the Ecumenical Movement it is the Commission of Faith and Order which has to look on behalf of the

[1] A question which naturally must arise in the context of the *munera*-doctrine.

whole movement into the central problem of how to overcome the deep rifts in the ways of self-understanding of the Churches. Naturally, some of the great items are the Ministry and the Sacraments. It is *naturally* so, because the great divergences of the different doctrines of the Church cluster around these points. But is it *properly* so? This question is valid for the simple reason that this absorbing occupation with the Ministry, its calling, its ordination, its authority, its training, betrays two things, often unrealized. First: that it is taken for granted that the "Ministry", i.e. the body of ordained "office-bearers" (German *Amtsträger*), is *the* body on which the Church depends and in which its real face appears. Second: in all these discussions on the "Ministry" the laity does not really rise above the horizon. The ecclesiologies, which pay great attention to the "universal priesthood of believers" and consequently to the laity, are doing so too exclusively in regard to the internal affairs of the Church, and its place and co-operation in them.

In adducing this example we do not intend in the least to gainsay the essential and abiding importance and indispensability of the "Ministry" in the sense of the ordained "office-bearers". That would be foolishness. What we want to signalize is the amazing absence of the laity as a substantial matter of consideration in the self-understanding of the Church. If one retorts that these "ministry-centred" discussions are a natural consequence of the undeniable fact that the Churches are forced to concentrate on this point of "the Ministry" as being one of the sore spots in the ecumenical discussion, I would answer: this is true, but nevertheless a distorted approach. It is not that different heritages from the past must find a common denominator; but a new vision of the Church, in which the laity gets its full meaning, must lead to a common new view of the meaning of the Ministry, or Clergy, as one aspect of the whole.[1]

When comparing the *central* emphasis on the priestly-hierarchical character of the Church in the Roman Catholic Church with the *strong* emphasis on the Ministry in the non-Roman episcopal and non-episcopal Churches, one cannot help feeling that the leaven of the former is still working in the latter. Many weighty historical reasons can be adduced to explain this. At present, however, we are called to rise above our historical imprisonments and limitations and rethink the nature, calling and implementation of the Church quite afresh. Three reasons at least make this imperative and also easier than in the past.

In the first place, our greater and surer knowledge of the relativities of history, which have played a rôle in the genesis and growth of our ecclesiologies and Church orders. The encumbrances of the past as well as its great gifts are more easily discernible.

In the second place, the call to unity embodied in the Ecumenical Movement obliges us to face the momentous question how to define anew, in our time, the permanent tension between the Church as a witnessing body of expectant pilgrims through history to God's End and Purpose, and the Church as an institution. The Church cannot but be *also* an institution.

---

[1] In the U.S.A., as part of a survey of the needs of theological training, H. Richard Niebuhr has published a book : *The Purpose of the Church and its Ministry*. This is indeed a book rich in mature wisdom. It is, however, amazing and also disappointing that in such a book, in which the rôle of the Church in American life is re-evaluated, the laity and its crucial significance in such a re-evaluation is hardly, if at all, mentioned.

But this is her perennial thorn in the flesh, because the Church is essentially "a colony of heaven", a divine new beginning on the earth and in the reality of the world, a "trek" and not an established institution. The institutional aspect is an indispensable apparatus, which should have its due place, but not the first place; for often (though certainly not always) it is like Saul's armour for David, an encumbrance and not a help.

When one studies, for example, the many papers in the Lund volume on the Nature of the Church, one realizes that our doctrines on the Church or Church orders are essentially theological justifications of the Churches as institutions. And when one reads, for instance, the Lambeth Quadrilateral, which plays such an important part as bridge-formula in ecumenical discussions, one realizes again the great extent to which our thinking on the Church is in terms of a well-balanced institution. Scripture, Creeds, Sacraments, and Episcopacy are in this important document the marks of the Church. One can agree with each of them as a proposition and nevertheless not have the feeling that the Church as the Reign of God's vivifying grace, of the power of Christ's hidden Kingship and of the working of the Holy Spirit, is primary. As items of negotiation (ominous word in the ecumenical vocabulary!) they evoke a different atmosphere. In practice the first and the second seem to cause no difficulty in Reunion negotiations. Only the third and fourth do, because there the doctrines of the Eucharist and the Ministry are involved. Yet it should be remarked that the little difficulty involved in the Creed shows how these negotiations are entirely an inner Church affair. The world, the present world with its quite different world-view, which obliges the Church

84

to rethink its historic thought forms, is out of sight. The only concern seems to be continuity with the past, not the relevance to the present and its new outlook. It neglects the fact that genuine continuity with the truth is a truer continuity than that with the expression of the past.

The recommendation which in Lund perhaps augured the best prospect for future ecumenical discussions is contained in the words: " In our work we have been led to the conviction that it is of decisive importance for the advance of ecumenical work that the doctrine of the Church be treated in close relation both to the doctrine of Christ and to the doctrine of the Holy Spirit."[1] This is a very appropriate but also a very risky recommendation. Risky in a good sense. Risky in this respect, that if not in the first place the doctrine of Christ and the Holy Spirit, as it is put in the quotation, but the sovereign *reality* and *claim* of Christ and the Holy Spirit on the Church, her spirit and life, were allowed to become the driving factors in the attempt at self-revision and new obedience, incalculable forces would enter which might change a theological commission into a Pentecost. New obedience to Christ and His Spirit, not better theology (unless the theology is the result of a new obedience) is creative.

In the third place, our time is one of well-nigh oppressive urgency. A new manifestation of the real nature and calling of the Church, in power and spirit, is demanded; not simply a restoration of the Church, or a Church more active in more directions than ever. The world unconsciously waits for the appearance of the Church in its true nature. *Renewal* of the Church

[1] *The Third World Conference on Faith and Order, Lund 1952,* p. 22.

is therefore the indispensable element, the *sine qua non* in all that happens, in the upsurge for unity, for evangelism etc. Renewal in the sense of the *perennial* imperative which accompanies always the life of the Church. In this sense the imperative is equally imperious for every kind of Church; the flourishing and the decadent ones, the self-complacent and the despondent. In the light of this rule of the perennial, constantly valid law of renewal, the laity, as said already, gets its essential place and meaning, because the *whole* Church is constantly called to renewal.[1] As we have got into the habit of not (as the Bible insists) considering Renewal the perennial and constant rule for the Church, but regard it as a miraculous episode which befalls us from time to time, self-assertion and self-affirmation are still very prominent in the confrontations of the Churches with each other, when they compare their credential letters, i.e. their ecclesiologies.

It cannot be denied that all our ecclesiologies, even those which are influenced by the idea of the universal priesthood of believers, reflect, by their whole architecture, institutions which answer to the overall definition of what a Church is, in O. Dibelius' book: *Das Jahrhundert der Kirche.*[2] This definition states that a Church is an organism which, as a peculiar form of religious life, contains a variety of people, is founded on a cult or form of worship and a creed, and whose unity and tradition are expressed in some kind of superior spiritual authority.

[1] See W. A. Visser 't Hooft: *The Renewal of the Church.*
[2] 1927; p. 97.

I am quite aware that all I have said above is certainly not all that can and should be said about our doctrines of the Church. They contain deeper tones and wider visions. In the face of the present challenging situation, however, it cannot be too often reiterated that the *primary* emphasis on the Church as an institution with creeds, sacraments and "orders", blocks at least at present the way to give first rank to the Church as an ever renewed adventure of faith, a response to God's great acts of salvation, redemption and reconciliation. The Church is not an end in itself, but a means to an end. And by "means" the Church in its *entirety* is meant, the laity as much as the "clergy". Faith as the ever new response to the reality of God in Christ, which implies ever new interpretation in confession[1] and conduct, not faith as a sum of doctrinal definitions of Christian truth, is what in most cases is meant in the Bible. This is not to say that faith (or better: belief) in the second sense has not its legitimate place. Of course it has. But again, it should not take first place; the more so, because faith as response is as essentially expressed in conduct as in confession. Or to put it theologically: dogmatics and ethics are two aspects of the same response of faith. It is one of the great merits of Karl Barth that he not only consistently keeps to this line in his great work, but has incorporated ethics quite naturally in his dogmatics. *Then*, the way opens up for a doctrine of the Church, which, without rejecting

---

[1] By confession is here, of course, meant not a credal statement, the Confessions we know from Church history, but the act of confessing. In fact, another word for "faith".

the indispensability of the institutional, does justice to the character of the Church as a herald of the new reality in Christ and of a new hope for the world, to the manifestation of which the *whole* membership of the Church is called.

Here again, the biblical stress on the perennial actuality of renewal of the Church gets its right perspective. One of the heritages from history which prevents us so often from seeing the Church, with all its greatness and misery, in its true light, is the distinction between the "empirical" and the "ideal" Church. It is to such a degree an element of our thinking that we hardly notice it. It has been since the first centuries a standard view, a means to give account of the, indeed, often disappointing state and quality of Christian faith and practice in the Church as it appeared. As such it is understandable; but nevertheless it proceeds more from the counsels of worldly wisdom than from the faith as response by which the Church should live, and the call to incessant renewal under which the Church stands as "God's own household", "*growing* into a holy temple in the Lord". However stubborn and refractory the stuff of ordinary reality may be —and it is—the Church, though with clear realism seeing this reality, can never permit itself to put the divine indicatives and imperatives, which are her peculiar directives and points of orientation, behind considerations which are properly speaking worldly in character.

In calling such considerations worldly, it is not meant to maintain that they are unreal. Far from that. They are frightfully real in human life, but yet they are not of *primary* relevance for the Church. For the Church does not live to wrest from empirical reality an "ideal" form of existence, but, obeying in faith the marching-orders which are inherent in its peculiar nature, waits for what will happen through this obedience in faith. For this reason the Church is indeed an "alien" body and has to represent this seemingly foolish and naïve "alienism". Because it lives by faith it cannot fall into line with either of the attitudes which obtain in the world: the so-called realistic, considered adjustment to a rather intractable world, or the idealistic striving for a more perfect order of life. The biblical note is to stress the *being* and *calling* of the Church, not as an ideal picture or ideal purpose, but as a reality in Christ which has to find embodiment in a peculiar and new order of existence.

NOT FITNESS—BUT RECREATIVE POWER

In the light of these elemental truths about the Church, Barth's[1] repudiation of another distinction, which has continually in history distorted the right view of the Church, seems to be correct, viz. the assumption that there are in the Church living and dead Christians, real and nominal Christians, useful and useless members. Nobody, of course, dreams of denying this empirical fact. Sects or movements which aim at freeing themselves from this annoyance by wanting to establish communities of true Christians only learn by experience that, after a period of apparent success with their endeavour, the same phenomena of converted and unconverted, of the grain and the tares, crop up. The point about these distinctions is not that they are not real, and can easily be

[1] *Church Dogmatics*, III/4, p. 560 in German edition.

waved aside, but that the approach to them is after the wisdom of the world and not after the peculiar wisdom of the Church. Barth's approach to it is to state as a truth inherent in the Gospel that in principle all Christians, to whatever category we may allot them, are unfit to be used by God, for the central stress lies in the Bible on our being called in spite of our unfitness. This may sound to many as rather lighthanded dealing with a desperate situation, a pious glossing over it. But in fact it puts every member, whether weak or strong, dead or alive, where he belongs, and it summons him to occupy the right place in regard to serving God's purpose: the place of humility and gratitude. If we have the faith to speak and act out of what the Church in Christ is, the whole problem of the laity gets a new, a full, face. It does not remain any more obscured by provisions and measures, through which in our ecclesiologies there is made more or less room for participation of the lay people in the functioning of the Church as an institution. The problem of the laity can only appear in its full stature, when the witness to what the Church is in its being and calling is made dependent not on the fitness of its members, but on the recreative power which is inherent in this being and calling and which concerns everybody, dead and alive alike. Nobody is "out of action". The Church in its totality is called and responsible, and so in this light the distinction between specially responsible and relatively non-responsible, however much on the surface seems to justify it, appears as an artificial distinction.[1]

Summarizing what has been said above on the question: is a theology of the laity possible?, not as an

[1] *Ibid.*

appendix to our existing ecclesiologies, but as an *organic part* of a total ecclesiology, the following points have appeared as essential. Only when the dimension of the world enters fully into the purview of a doctrine of the Church, when the perennial call for renewal is fully accounted for in it and when the directives for the Church's life and expression are taken from the Church's being and calling, fully aware of the risk of faith this implies, is a genuine theology of the laity (as an indispensable part of the whole doctrine of the Church) possible. If one of these three is lacking, it is of course nevertheless possible to develop a theology of the laity, but it will then occupy a more or less supplementary position to a differently orientated ecclesiology.

This it is, according to my view, that is at stake in Congar's words quoted at the beginning of this chapter: "Au fond, il n'y aurait qu'une théologie du laïcat valable: une ecclésiologie totale." The underlying questions are always: What is the Church? What is the Church for? If that is not kept in mind, the lay ministry, about which so much is being said at present, remains on the level of a many-sided activity in which the self-assertion of the laity threatens to be more evident than a new manifestation of the Church in modern society. The responsible participation of the laity in the discharge of the Church's divine calling is not primarily a matter of idealism and enthusiasm or organizational efficiency, but of a new grasp of and commitment to the meaning of God's redemptive purpose with man and with the world, in the past, the present, and the future: a purpose which has its foundation and inexhaustible content in Christ, God incarnate, who died for us on the Cross and rose from the dead. It is of vital importance to keep these three: incarnation, crucifixion, and resurrection, equally in the centre. They must always be held together. There is always a tendency to centre on one of them, on a theology of the Incarnation, of the Cross, or of the Resurrection, not so much at the expense of the other two (as they are of course by no means denied) but nevertheless to centre the whole meaning of the Christian faith around one of the three, with the result that the full richness of the total Gospel is diminished. Each of the three aspects of God's coming into the world is meaningless without the other two. The incarnation and the crucifixion are in the first place acts of humility and obedience on Jesus' part, revealing the heart of God (Phil. 2:8); not a raising of human nature into the divine nature, but to open a way to a new life of new obedience and hope in the light of the cross and the resurrection. A theology of the laity in this connection means the appropriation of the significance of God's revelation in Christ for our thinking, our attitudes, our decisions and actions.

This is not "professional" theology. This is every Christian's job. Canon Demant has made this very clear in his excellent book *Theology of Society*, especially in regard to the Anglo-Saxon situation. He says:[1] "It is still a common practice in England and America to speak of the Church as the body that exists to give the world its moral and social ideals, and also a kind of powerhouse to put enough spiritual energy behind the best-meaning projects of society". The whole assumption, he goes on to say in that chapter,[2] is that religion should be of use, a practical religion. The Church should "cease trying to give a better

[1] p. 148.   [2] Aptly called: "The mischief of ideals".

92

answer than the world to the problems the world has set in its own way. It must take the problems men have and show that they are insoluble unless they are restated in terms of the nature of the reality as the Christian faith knows it."[1] The Church, Demant urges, is not there to dispense principles and ideals, but to announce affirmations about the nature of reality, the nature of God, of man, etc. He stresses, as we have done above, that the faith which conquered the world did not proclaim ideals. It testified first to an "is" and then it became power for an "ought". "The faith that has moved men has always been an indicative before it was an imperative."[2] The Christian religion, Demant reminds us,[3] is a religion of redemption, that is to say of liberation; it is a gospel. It is good news, not good advice. The good news is that God, source, end and Lord of the created world, is by His own divine initiative active to restore things to their true nature, and invites men to enter into this stream of divine liberation. The whole membership of the Church is by the fact of its membership through baptism in principle within the stream of the invited. A theology of the laity, developed with this background in mind, can be a great help in realizing this and its consequences in all the grandeur, sacrifice and suffering this may entail.

"PRIESTHOOD OF BELIEVERS"—A CRITIQUE

When thinking about the possibility of a theology of the laity as an integral part of the testimony of the Church about its own meaning, it seems very obvious to start from the thesis of the "universal priesthood of

[1] p. 149.　　[2] pp. 150, 151.　　[3] p. 11.

believers" as one of the precious, but insufficiently developed, legacies of the Reformation. It is often done in the new thinking which in the last decade has blossomed forth around the place and participation of the laity. W. Robinson in his lectures on " Completing the Reformation, the Doctrine of the Priesthood of all Believers "[1] presents one of these attempts, in which, however, fortunately the focal point is that the " vocation " of the layman is as deeply " religious " as that of the priest, and that, in fact, it is too a priestly vocation.[2] Various ecclesiologies (e.g. the Baptist) put great stress on it.

It is true that the priesthood of the believers is good biblical doctrine, or, to phrase it differently, it is inherent in the being of the Church, God's people. It is also true that the priesthood of believers, as the Bible presents it, has to be one of the ferments of a theology of the laity. Yet I would dissuade from taking it as a starting-point. For, try as we may, when it is developed as the word for the *present* situation, this development involuntarily remains conditioned by the historical reminiscences that accompany this thesis of the universal priesthood. The insistence on it as the key to understanding the meaning of the laity seems to me ill-advised, because it is a too partial approach. Moreover, it has acquired more and more an individualistic accent, wholly alien and even contrary to the biblical notion which is " the priesthood of the whole Church ". At the time of the Reformation it was not only a new discovery of biblical truth, but it was above all a cry of protest against a Church wholly ruled by priestcraft. It was at the same time a protest

[1] Spring Lectures 1955 at the College of the Bible, Lexington (Ky.).
[2] p. 15.

against the ascetic perfectionist ideal of the true Christian life, which was sanctioned by the Church, and which robbed the lives of ordinary Christians of inner value and meaning. In the doctrine of the "universal priesthood of believers" there was an attempt to put right the distorted relation of "secular" and "religious" vocation. This character of protest, often expressed, especially by Luther, in such strong affirmations and claims that they could not but break down on the stubborn realities of life, has lent to the doctrine of the "universal priesthood of believers" a tendency towards a plea for lay religion and lay revolt, towards disinterestedness in the Church as the "household of God" (Eph. 2:19). In this way, the case of the laity is too exclusively determined by the opposition to Rome, which appears from the word "priestly". The case of the laity should at present not be envisaged mainly from this Rome-determined angle, but from a fuller biblical perspective. The "universal priesthood of believers" narrows the range of the "new creation" the Church is meant to represent. The issue is not that, if the laity were only given the opportunity and the right to do so, they would come to the rescue of the Church. The issue is that both laity and ministry stand in need of a new vision of the nature and calling of the Church and their *distinctive places* in it, which means conversion and reformation for the whole Church, laity as well as ministry. Renewal is always based on repentance and new commitment and dedication to the fundamental basis of Christian existence, viz. God's craving for the collaboration with Him of His whole Church, in His work of redemption.

THE ORTHODOX CHURCH *"PLEROMA"*—
A CRITIQUE

The Orthodox Churches often emphasize in ecumenical discussions that one of the main points in
their understanding of the Church is: Clergy and laity
make together the fulness (*pleroma*) of the Church
and the expression of its authority through the conscience of the Church, i.e. the common mind both of
clergy and laymen, and in the sense of "id tenemus
quod ubique, quod semper, quod ab omnibus creditum
est ".[1]   This point expresses the particular concern of
the Orthodox Church to give first rank to the conception of the Church as community, and not as a body
of hierarchical authority. This "unitotality" or "uni-
plurality" of the Church has received a specifically
strong emphasis in the discussion around the Russian
word "sobornost", a term which owes its popularity
to a number of great Slavophile writers. It claims to
express the special genius of Oriental Orthodoxy. It
means to say that the believer only exists and that
truth only reveals itself to him in the living community
of the whole Church. Further, that truth is no external
authority but is an inner light and that neither bishops
nor Councils have authority in the field of truth.[2]

The reason we bring this piece of Orthodox ecclesiology (of which the idea of the "sobornost" is more
the particular theory of this group of Russian thinkers
than Orthodox doctrine) into our discussion on the

[1] "What has been believed everywhere, all the time, by everyone—that we hold." See *The Nature of the Church*, edited by
R. Newton Flew, pp. 48, 53.

[2] See the illuminating discussion of this whole matter in Congar,
op. cit., pp. 380-386.

possibility of a theology of the laity is that this proclamation of the clergy and laity, making together the
fulness of the Church, is often presented as the solution
to the problem of the right relation of clergy and laity
in the Church, and, as such, the right theological
definition of the laity; also for the present attempts to
formulate such a theology. It is only fair to ask: is
this right or not? It is too little known that in the
Orthodox Church outstanding laymen have often an
influential rôle, particularly in the field of theology
and religious instruction. There is a great amount of
lay activity, pressing for renewal of Church life, often
without that close clerical supervision and direction
which characterizes the Roman Catholic Church. It
seems to us, however, that the real interest in Orthodox
thinking is not focused on the problem of Church and
World and on the Church Militant in a world which
has become alienated from the Christian faith. It is
rather one of the characteristics of the Orthodox world
that it never has really seen and faced the problem of
Church and World. It leaves the world to its own
devices. Its interest lies in the being of the Church.
The calling of the Church in regard to the world lies
outside the horizon. The affirmation that the clergy
and the laity make together the fulness of the Church
is, so to speak, above all an act of self-contemplation of
the Church, directed to the past in order to demonstrate the unbroken continuity of the Orthodox Church
with the undivided Church.[1]

This is the central concern of the Orthodox Church,
because on it is founded its claim to be the only one
and true Church amidst all the Churches. The continuity with the past is undoubtedly in the ongoing

[1] Cf. *The Nature of the Church*, p. 48.

ecumenical discourse a theme of great importance, as it touches one's view of the nature of the Church. A genuine theology of the laity is, however, only possible when both the nature and the calling of the Church, of the ek-*klèsia*, are grasped as equally significant and essential. To live as a Christian *in* the world, to be the Church *in* the world, requires a resolute orientation and interest in the present and the future, more than in the past, as the Church has to demonstrate her authenticity by being "steadfast and unmovable, always abounding in the work of the Lord" (1 Cor. 15:58).

Chapter 4

PRELUDE TO A THEOLOGY OF THE LAITY

THE whole gamut of new, stirring awareness and inner disturbance, manifested in a revival of apostolic sensitivity; of experiments in new Christian living and evangelism; of new, stimulating theological thinking; of new visions of the Church and its "why" and "for what"; of inner disturbance about the scandal of disruption of the Church and the longing for a more unambiguous manifestation of its oneness; of the manifold aspects of the deep concern about the laity and its participation in the expression of the reality of the Church; is the sure indication of a rising feeling that a radical Reformation of the Church is due. Probably more radical than the Reformation of the 16th century, because the pressure both of the Spirit and of the world are upon us to rethink and reshape the response to the divine calling of the Church. This is not to say that we can dispose and construe a reformation, but that we see its necessity and work for it.

It is the serious conviction of the present writer that in such a reformation the laity has to play a decisive rôle. Not on account of its special ability, but because of its strategical place in the present predicament of the Church in a world which has lost all sense of the reality of God and His order of life. Everything in the Church and in the world revolves around the so-called "ordinary member of the Church". For in him must become somehow visible that the Lordship of Christ over the Church and over the world is not a fairy-tale or a gratuitous assertion, but a reality which "bites". The apparatus of the Church has to be directed towards that end. Not towards the maintenance of historical institutions and formulations, as if they are sacrosanct and inviolable. The total activity of the Church in its worship, its preaching, its teaching, its pastoral care, should have the purpose of helping the "ordinary membership of the Church" to become what they are in Christ.

This would signify already a radical reformation. By God's grace we live in a time of rediscovery of the Church and of the wholeness of the Church. We see more clearly than often has been the case that ecclesiology and christology are one. The ekklèsia, the community of believers, has as its first and foremost qualification that it is *that community*, which *as community* belongs to Christ and is in Christ, and as such is the sphere of God's salvation, redemption and reconciliation and of Christ's rulership. This is the archetypal reality of the Church. To see and seize this essential point is a great blessing. This blessing, however, could as well become a curse, if it remained a theme of theological meditation and self-contemplation. This new knowledge is not real knowledge, if it is not accompanied by a horror about the alienation of the empirical Church from its own fundamental reality and by a deep longing for a tangible manifestation of the Church's true nature. This horror and this longing are the deeper motives which are operating in many of the events and passionate discussions around the place and responsibility of the laity as an organic part of the Church.

THE WHOLE MEMBERSHIP

Therefore, a theology of the laity has to be a contribution to and an explanation of this archetypal reality or true dimension of the Church and of its calling to show forth the powers of the Kingdom of God. These latter words are another way of saying that the Church in its whole membership is that peculiar body in which the Lordship of Christ is an experienced and demonstrated reality and in which the faith in His Lordship over the world is a dynamic for unremitting witness and action. This must be said with special stress, because the Lordship of Christ in the Church is in a number of our ecclesiologies an avowed *principle of Church-government* pointing towards the true dimension of the Church, but in practice not a motive force.

In our time a theology of the laity has to be to a certain degree also a theology for the laity, for if the word "laity" is taken seriously it includes not only the already active awakened and spiritually intelligent ordinary members of the Church. It includes *everybody*, men and women, rich and poor, socially outstanding and inconspicuous, well-educated and less-educated, in short all the categories under which the membership of the Church can be distributed. The Apostle Paul in his Epistles does so without hesitation. He addresses himself to "churches", consisting of recent converts, and as a pastor and builder of these young, new "churches" he enters into their actual problems, deviations and confusions. In doing so, he introduces them with great profundity to the full scope of God's reality in Christ and the new world of truth, value and power this represents, interspersing it with manifold advice of Christian common sense. He does so, unconcerned about the fact that he deals with the "weak" and the "strong", the "mean" and "despised" in the world, the "wise" and the "boasters" or the "babes" in Christ. Rather he relishes doing so, because they are altogether the "Church", the domain or the dominion of Christ and His Spirit. The domain and dominion of Christ and His Spirit is the determinant, not the available or not available amount of the understanding of the Christians. The laity as it is, not a "select" laity, must always be in our mind. There often exists, amongst those who work hard at getting the lay issue in the right perspective, a dangerous tendency to think only in terms of a "select" laity. Of course a certain minority of the laity, who possess great cultural and educational advantages or occupy important places in some sector of the world's life, have, if this is truly brought under the rule of Christ, special significance. But in the first place, the rule must stand that the whole laity matters, of whatever description, both the "select" and the ordinary laity. Both are called.

This biblical example should be regulative. To-day in many respects we are in the same situation as the Primitive Church. The laity, the ordinary membership of the Church, is to a great extent ignorant and spiritually illiterate. On account of a certain fidelity, apparent in regular churchgoing and participation in Church activities, this spiritual illiterarcy is largely overlooked. It is very unrealistic to think that the laity in its majority has any adequate idea of the tremendous purport of such keywords as redemption, reconciliation, Kingdom of God, forgiveness of sins, the foolishness of the Cross. In various countries and "churches" there may be some variety in the degree of spiritual illiteracy. The most telling example is perhaps America, maybe for the reason that people there are in the good habit of investigating into such matters. America is at present the scene of an unprecedented upsurge of religion, of return to the Churches. In order to make quite plain what we mean by "spiritual illiteracy" and its implications and concomitants, which operate everywhere in the world of the Churches, we will quote from W. Herberg's book, *Protestant, Catholic, Jew*:[1]

"In the five years from 1949 to 1953 the distribution of Scriptures in the United States increased 140 per cent, reaching an all-time high of 9,726,391 volumes a year. People were apparently buying and distributing the Bible at an unprecedented rate. Furthermore, over four-fifths of adult Americans said they believed the Bible to be 'the revealed word of God' rather than merely a 'great piece of literature'. Yet, when these same Americans were asked to give the 'names of the first four books of the New Testament', 53 per cent could not name even one. The Bible can hardly be said to enter into the life and thought of Americans quite as much as their views on its divine inspiration and their eagerness to buy and distribute it might suggest. . . . The people who join the Churches, take part in Church activities . . . are honest intelligent people who take their religion quite seriously". Yet their religious thinking, feeling and acting "do not bear an unequivocal relation to the faith they profess". It is "religiousness in a secularist framework". This quotation, which inevitably has some American undertones, nevertheless helps us to make it mercilessly clear that

[1] pp. 14, 15.

a theology of the laity must also be in a certain sense a theology for the laity, an eye-opener to what the Christian faith and the Church are really about.

It must, therefore, bear the mark of simplicity, free from the technicalities of professional theology.[1] It nevertheless is theology, because every piece of coherent Christian thinking on the meaning and scope of the Christian Revelation and Faith is theology. As such, theology is not the special concern of a specialized group, but the business of *every* Christian.[2]

These realistic remarks have to be prefaced to a concise outline of a theology of the laity in order to make us aware of the paradoxical situation in which we find ourselves. On the one hand to maintain that the greatest strategical point in a serious attempt at the renewal and reformation of the Church, is the laity, the laity as a whole, not a "select" laity, seemingly fitted for the purpose. On the other hand, to stress that the common laity in all its variety is, worldly speaking, to a great extent very inept material because of its far-going spiritual illiteracy and self-diffidence. The example of our Lord in the Gospels and of Paul's praxis in his Epistles encourages us, however, to accept this paradoxical situation, and to understand that, from

[1] This is not said to depreciate professional theology, which if it is pursued not for its own sake, but for the service of the Church and the world, is of inestimable worth. It is. however, even in this case in danger of being often a frustrating bogey to lay people, strengthening their feeling of inability.

[2] It is disappointing that Congar in his book expressly states (p. 430): "Theology in its proper sense can only be 'savoir de prêtres', because the laity is not inserted in the dogmatic tradition of the Church in the same way as the priest. The laity's contribution to theology is of secondary order, not because of their lesser amount of learning and erudition which belong to the professional theologian, but because of their 'status' in the Church."

the background of the Gospel, it is even not paradoxical at all. To treat systematically ordinary Church members as immature, keeps them immature. Our second chapter has clearly shown that. It is a fact of faith, inherent in the presence of Christ and His Spirit in the Church, and also a fact of experience that Christ is able to create out of all kinds of people, men and women, independent, responsible people, who know that they are called. *Provided* what is spoken to them is said on the basis of real faith, of the presence of Christ and His Spirit in the Church, of whatever description it may be. In the so-called foreign mission-field new, living, spiritually intelligent congregations are built out of very immature, ignorant people. There is to be sure a place for "milk" and "meat", but this is not a distinction made in order to justify not addressing plainly all lay people on what they *are* in principle— servants of Christ; and on what they are called to become and to be—wholehearted members of the great fellowship in Christ. This seeming digression is not superfluous, because it is still largely the custom in the life of the Churches to approach its membership of very different substance on the basis of their supposed amount of willingness, unwillingness, or unfitness, and not straightforwardly on the basis of their being called.

APOSTLES' CREED—OATH OF ALLEGIANCE

Let us begin to make some observations around the Apostles' Creed and the Lord's Prayer, two permanent elements of the liturgies of all Churches.

It is not necessary to agree whether the Apostles' Creed is the most satisfactory and comprehensive summary of the Christian Faith. Some doubt is justified here, in the face of the strange fact that on the one hand its liturgical use and the insistence on its summarizing the Catholic Faith are universally agreed to, whereas on the other hand the sophistication of "professional" theology about some of its articles is equally on the increase. The essential thing, in our case, to seize in regard to it is that at the time of its origin and subsequent use it served as an excellent baptismal oath of allegiance to the Church as the fellowship of those who had, in the midst of a hostile world, opted for Jesus Christ as the Lord of their life. It was a *sacramentum* in the original sense of the word, that is, the oath of allegiance of a soldier to his commander; in this case, the declaration that one entered the *militia Christi*, thereby leaving the old world to which one had belonged, the world of untruth and death, and entering the *new* world of the Church with her quite different law of life. The act of Baptism dramatized this transition from "darkness" to "light", from old to new, in a brief form, because this act meant to symbolize, to express the incorporation into and with Christ, His death and resurrection (Rom. 6:3, 4). The basis of entering the membership of the Church was (and is) the acts of God, done in and through Jesus Christ. Membership of the Church is a privilege, a divine favour.

In this light the Apostles' Creed in its remarkable terseness becomes transparent. One was (and is) baptized in the name of the Father, the Son and the Holy Spirit. "I believe in God the Father, in Jesus Christ, His Son, *our Lord*, and in the Holy Spirit", is the kernel, the core of the Apostles' Creed. To say that the Church is of God (1 Cor. 1:2) is the same as to say that it is the Church of Christ ("the called of Jesus Christ", Rom. 1:6) or the Church of the Spirit. It is patent that in this threefold confession the heart of the matter lies in the lapidary facts enumerated under the confession of faith in Jesus Christ, *our Lord*. The crux and the glory of Christianity is that it is a historic faith. Faith, not in a myth, an ideology, an idealistic scheme of self-salvation and self-fulfilment designed by men, but in an event in history, dated and all. An intervention of God Himself, the turning-point of all history with a new outlook and new hope for the Reign of God. The oldest confession, "*Jesus is the Lord*" (1 Cor. 12:3) sharpens this point of the historic basis. Jesus, the man of Nazareth, who suffered under Pontius Pilate in A.D. 29, is the Lord. Allegiance to Him is the prime matter, for the believers "are called into the fellowship of His Son Jesus Christ our Lord" (1 Cor. 1:9), into "the fellowship of the Spirit" (Phil. 2:1). The Nicene Creed rightly speaks of "the Holy Spirit, the Lord and Giver of life". That is the *locus standi* of the Church, under the Lordship of Christ and the Spirit. All other lordship in the Church is either illegitimate or subordinate or subservient. That is the fundamental law of the new world.

The second point that needs special mention for our purpose is that the Church is also an article of faith, the one brotherhood in Christ, the new world, which is "holy", that is: separated from the old world, its spirit and works. The fellowship (*koinonia*) with and in Jesus Christ and the Spirit is the creative ground and sustainer of the fellowship (*koinonia*) of the believers with each other. *Therefore* the oneness of the Church is inviolable, irremovable, and its apparent disruption in our denominationalism a riddle and a scandal. Not because of the ability to fellowship (*koinonia*) in the Christians is the oneness of the Church guaranteed and sealed. If this "fellowship" were the first and main thing it would be unreasonable to believe in the oneness of the Church. Rather because we have treated and still often treat *our* "fellowship" as the first and real thing, insufficiently awed by and obedient to its creative ground, the biblically speaking unnatural, even impossible, disruption and disunity is such a stubborn fact.

THE LORD'S PRAYER—FRATERNAL SOLIDARITY

The Lord's Prayer also gives occasion for some remarks in order to show up some ingredients of ecclesiological importance. The fate that has befallen it, viz. to become mainly a liturgical prayer, has to a great extent killed its inherent power.[1] This holds true, even when we do not want to forget that the performance of praying it as a liturgical act is often hallowed by sacred and genuine emotion. It is, the more one tries to penetrate into its meaning, an amazing combination of simplicity and profundity, of brief directness and naturalness. It is really elemental and startling, when one ponders on it, or makes the praying of it an elevating and purifying exercise of heart and mind. Truly startling is the prayer to forgive our trespasses as we forgive those who have trespassed against us. It seems very unorthodox to make our

[1] Not so long ago, when I had led a chapel service which I ended by praying the Lord's Prayer, one of the participants came afterwards excited to me, saying: "This is the first time in my life I have realized that the Lord's Prayer is not a liturgical act, but a prayer, because you prayed it and did not recite it."

readiness to forgive the precondition of God's readiness to do so; the more because the Bible speaks in such strong terms of God (cf. for example Psalm 103, Isaiah 1 and the Parable of the Prodigal Son). Yet it is wholly consonant with the dominant note, ringing through the whole Sermon on the Mount, in which the Lord's Prayer is inserted: be and do in such or such a way, because God is and does so. And is there a more effective way to express that forgiveness is not God's *métier* but His disposition?

Still more startling is the sequence, the hallowing of God's Name, the coming of God's Reign, the doing of His will in heaven and on earth, etc. In all its elusive simplicity it flashes out and unveils the fundamental trouble of the world of men with its conflicting wills and its non-conformity of will with God's Will, and also "the saving health" (Ps. 67) which is only safe in the hands of the Most High. Dante in his *Paradiso* was certainly taught by it when he said: "Nella sua volontà è nostra pace".[1] And yet, this prayer with this grand sweep begins homely: *Our* Father. And throughout it is: give *us*, forgive *us*, deliver *us*. It is the prayer of the family of God. Jesus has come to found a family, a family *above* and *out* of all families. The Church is meant as a family. The "we-thou" has precedence over the "I-thou" —which is often forgotten when we try to formulate our understanding of man. When the multitude warns Him that His mother and brothers want to stop Him, He says: "Who is my mother or my brethren?" and looking on those who were sitting around Him, He said: "These are my brothers and my mother. *Whosoever* does the will of God, is my brother and my

[1] " In His will is our peace."

sister and mother" (Mark 3:31-35). Therefore Jesus says: "Where two or three are gathered in my Name, I am in the midst of them." But always as the Lord, however so much He is the Companion and the Head of the family. This Lordship pierces through the severe words: "Whosoever loves father or mother above me, is unworthy of me."

This family-character of the Church must have consequences for the quality and tone of life it exhibits. Our Church orders and ecclesiologies seem to have little or no room for this category of the Church, although there are signs of renewal, in spite of our "orders", in the increasing urge to manifest a conduct of fraternal solidarity and to seek the practice of Christian familyhood in small groups, as for instance the house-churches, which are consciously conceived after the pattern of the New Testament.

In making these few observations in relation to the Apostles' Creed and the Lord's Prayer, we have merely opened up some glimpses of the Church's meaning to indicate what tremendous claims and promises are inherent in the Church, touching the whole range of history and of man's life, if it really understands itself as the Church of Jesus Christ, the Renewer of the world and of man, the Healer of its diseases, the Inaugurator of a new humanity. The claims and promises are indeed so tremendous that if the Church did it in its own name and right, it would be blasphemy. It can only witness to its Lord, to whom these claims and purposes belong, and (which is extremely important) has to show the fruits of its recognition of these claims in its "living and moving", for it is for the Church itself in the first place that the words "Whosoever shall do the will of God" were spoken.

If these fruits are not forthcoming, it is a result of the lack of "vigilance" of the whole Church in all its members. It makes the Church uncertain and uneasy in its witness. Hence this perennial call for renewal that has to ring through the Church, to which we previously alluded. For a sound conception of and sound attitude to the Church it is of vital significance to keep this common guilt of all the members well in mind. That alone is the right family spirit, which brings us to a new awareness that a Church, when in weakness, decay and unfaithfulness, can only become a genuine *koinonia* (fellowship) again by groping jointly back to the creative ground of the Christian *koinonia*, viz. the *koinonia* in and with Christ and the Holy Spirit.

Becoming or being a member of the Church was, as we indicated, primarily a matter of faithful allegiance to the Lord or to the Family Head, Jesus Christ, firmly believing in God the Father, the Son and the Holy Spirit as the truly creative and sustaining realities and powers in the universe.

We children of our time have to be the Church in a totally different world and atmosphere. In the first centuries of her existence the Church with her strange claims and loyalties was offensive. At present, in that respect, the world offers a contradictory spectacle. In the "Western" world the Church is not offensive at all. It is an institution with a long history and tradition, considered to "belong" to the picture of Western civilization, whose Roman-Greek and Hebrew-Christian roots are readily acknowledged. In the official climate of religious liberty and tolerance the Church can quietly continue its life as it thinks fit, provided it be not offensive and does not meddle with the general affairs of the world in a way that is not considered "useful". But this same Western civilization in which the Church (in its essence a "colony of heaven", the herald and instrument of God's invasion in the world) functions, is bewilderingly self-contradictory. It is not unmindful of its roots and of the moral fibre and creative impulses grown out of them, but at the same time it lives and behaves without any sense of a transcending order of life. It lives and behaves as if the tremendous assertions of the Christian Faith were irrelevant. This self-contradictory Western civilization is, however, under way to shake and mould the peoples of Asia and Africa, where the "Younger Churches" live as representatives of the Church.

The "Eastern world", in the present political sense of the word, shows a picture which is quite different. There the Church is again in the state of being an "offence", the last enemy to be overcome on the road to a free, religionless world. As institution it is still reckoned with, treated with various grades of sufferance, according to the shifting requirements of political expedience.

The "Western world" lives and lets live. The effect of this seemingly ideal condition is that this Western world is, in fact, from the standpoint of the Church's being and calling, of its vocation to witness to and reflect the divine order of life, the most dangerous spot for the Church to live in. The most dangerous, because it is constantly tempted to function as an ingredient and not as the salt of the world. Therefore, one of the most needed requisites of a renewal of the Church is to see through this temptation. In the "Eastern world" it is one monolithic ideology that strives to prevail. It lives, but does not let live, unless the outsiders bend to its service. Essentially, Communism is the most intolerable pseudo-Church that ever was. In regard to the Church, according to circumstances it persecutes, suppresses, vexes or seduces. Speaking on principle, that is on the basis of a true self-understanding of the Church, of its being and calling, the Church is there not in the most dangerous, but in the most *clearly* challenging spot of the world. The temptation is not, as in the West, to fail to discern the challenge, but to evade it and to refuse to take upon herself suffering as a privilege. It seems very complacent and facile to say such an enormous thing, but it is said out of the desire to put things in their proper biblical perspective, where suffering for Christ's sake is not artificially sought for, but when it comes is accepted "for even hereunto were ye called (Moffatt translates: it is your vocation) because Christ also suffered for us, leaving us an example that ye should follow His footsteps" (1 Peter 2:21).

THE LAITY IN THE ENCOUNTER

These brief remarks are written, not as an attempt to analyse the present world situation, but to suggest that the Church is functioning to-day in an uncongenial (West) or hostile world (East). In principle this is always the case, but at present it is more apparent or at least more demonstrable. The laity, more than the ministry, are immersed in this situation and have to come to grips with it. Undoubtedly the theologians have greater intellectual knowledge of it, because their work obliges them to interpret the Message in relation and correlation with or in contradiction to the thinking outside the Church. Nevertheless, it is the laity, living and working in the world, which daily experiences the deep gulf between what the Church stands for and what the world drives at. They are moulded, mangled, confused or suffocated by the dominant trends of thought. Many are bewildered; also many develop a schizophrenic type of mind, harbouring two incompatibles in their thinking, delegating the Christian Faith and what it is about to an innocuous Sunday-department of life, and so losing the acute sensitivity of what the Christian Faith and Church are really about. Few struggle and conquer a new awareness of the peculiar relevance of the Christian Faith and Church to this modern world as well. It is just on the point of enabling the laity to account for the hope and the faith which is in them that the theologians have to meet and strengthen the laity. Provided they let themselves also be taught by the laity. For the laity should in this matter not be seen primarily as the needy, ignorant and helpless, but as that part of the Church that has to carry the brunt of the burden of encounter with the world in and around themselves, and to voice and incarnate the Church's or better, Christ's relevance, to the whole range of human life. If not, words like Paul's bold saying to Timothy (1 Tim. 3 : 15) about " the Church of the *living* God, the pillar and bulwark of the truth " sound, in fact, like an empty, even ridiculously arrogant declamation and not like a believable tenet.

An attempt to try to determine the place and part of the laity in the whole life expression of the Church in an outline of a theology of the laity should show awareness of the fact that it is done at a time in which it seems a foolhardy undertaking. To spin beautiful thoughts in the air and call that a theology of the laity will not do. Therefore our remarks about a *mutual* co-operation of theologians and lay people, in which both are teachers and taught, touch a vital point. It is too much the habit of theologians to have a lively discussion amongst themselves and often only fully understandable to them.[1] To be sure, this has its due place. But when (as it should be) they enter the arena of our confused world, the counsel and co-operation of a great variety of lay people are a requisite for helping to make the ministry of the Church more effective. Or, to put it differently, it should belong to the well-considered strategy of the Church to make such counsel and co-operation a new habit. For many of these lay people live and struggle in this confused world, seeking for the way to see and to express the deep relevance of the Christian Faith to the world, in which they happen to live. They therefore need help in order to feel really like *milites*, who keep loyalty to their oath of allegiance. But they not only need help. They can and should render good service by their more acute experience of actual life and by their often greater knowledge of the real perplexities a Christian, called to commit himself in his peculiar circumstances to the service of the Lord Jesus Christ, has to face. In the World Council of Churches we fortunately see signs of

[1] The resurrection of the *vocal* type of lay theologian in some European countries is very significant. I think (to confine myself to England) e.g. about C. S. Lewis. Theologians especially should be mindful of the fact that his books, which combine apology and attack, reach far more people than the books of a great number of theologians together. A somewhat different example are the books by C. E. M. Joad (e.g. *The Present and Future of Religion* and *Recovery of Belief*), who as an erstwhile influential philosophical freethinker describes how he has found out that this "strange Christian belief" gives the most satisfactory view of human reality.

this counsel and co-operation, and here and there in Churches, but it is also true that in the World Council the tendency to draw in the laity is still far too weak.

These remarks do not yet in the least compass the problem in its full range. They compass a small part of it, viz. the intellectual, cultural aspect of the present conjunction of Church and World. However, it should be kept in mind that the lay Christian of the first centuries, for whom his confession of faith was at the same time his oath of allegiance, did it in a quite different atmosphere from the lay Christian of to-day, for whom his avowal of faith should be equally his oath of allegiance to the cause of Jesus Christ in the world. Although the world of basic realities to which the Church then witnessed was a very " strange ", unusual world, yet it was a world in which the necessity and naturalness of a hallowing of life in all its aspects was instinctively recognized and in which salvation, atonement, redemption (about which the Christian Church spoke, and has always to speak, with great urgency) were frenetically desired and sought. We move in a quite different world, with quite different preoccupations. The standard of living, the increased effectiveness of production, the heightening of comfort—to mention only a few of the dominant preoccupations—rule the mind. Many of the best people often put the anxious question: is it really possible to live as a Christian in this world of exclusive this-worldly preoccupation and of threatening self-destruction, which hangs as a heavy cloud above all this feverish activity? By the irrepressible march of technics and mastery of nature the immediacy of God is simply killed. It seems a silly, antiquated idea. The self-reliance engendered by the experience that, as it seems, man can manage his own business fairly well, practically seems to rule out the possibility of taking the reality of God seriously. The new geological and astronomical time-scales, which quite naturally have invaded the mind of every thinking person, confront us with a radical rethinking of our faith in God the Creator and Sustainer of everything. They relegate the story about the Creation a hundred times more to the realm of poetry than the discovery that it is not a historical account has done.

One could go on for a long time adding other instances. The point that has to be made, however, is that the powerful suggestion which radiates from the modern view of life and the world seems to make vigorous religious life impossible or anaemic. And yet the Christian Church is called to a *vigorous* witness, and its laity has to play a very significant rôle in the midst of this life, in its sublimity and its degradation, because that cannot be left to sermons and official proclamations. We must realize that because of the weakness and hesitancy in the expression of their faith —a weakness and hesitancy which in the uncongenial atmosphere of a one-dimensional world is not amazing —in confrontation with the present sense of life and the world, the laity is not able to fulfil its calling as part of the Church.

There is hardly a tone of victory and joy, or evidence of a life of joy in the midst of great stress, which distinguishes the Christian community from all other communities. Yet, joy in the Holy Spirit is the basic spirit of the Bible. Quotations are superfluous. One may stand for many. The first Epistle of Peter is written to Christians living in the dispersion (*diaspora*). It is clear from its context that their life is a very hard one. But the Epistle begins with a deep note of great joy: "Blessed be the God and Father of our Lord Jesus Christ who according to His abundant mercy hath begotten us again unto a living hope by the resurrection of Jesus Christ from the dead". In order to regain an "adult Christianity" an immersion in the Bible and its direct, unambiguous way of speaking about God and His centrality is indispensable for the Church as a whole. Especially indispensable for the laity, if they are to be enabled to become what they are often called nowadays: the spearhead of the Church, and not its hesitant rearguard. The first and great commandment: "Thou shalt love the Lord thy God with all thy *heart*, and with all thy *soul* and with all thy *mind*" (Matthew 22: 37) is imperative for the whole membership of the Church, not for a tiny part, and the whole membership should accordingly be approached on that basis. The last words, "with all thy mind", have nowadays, for the laity particularly, a special significance on account of the powerful suggestions which emanate from the modern view of life, to which allusion has been made.

The real issue is: are we part of a blind universe (for a universe without God is blind) which inexplicably moves towards the perfect man (as many believe), provided it be not overtaken by the catastrophe of self-destruction, or are we part of a universe of which the living God, the Father of our Lord Jesus Christ, is the centre, the Creator and Sustainer, leading it to *His* end, even when the catastrophe of self-destruction overtakes us? For it is not our anxious, sometimes agonizing calculations, legitimate as they may be in our insecure yet security-thirsting world, that can be the pole-star of the Christian Church, but the world of triumphant faith of Romans 8:38, 39: "For I am certain neither death nor life, neither angels nor principalities, neither the present *nor the future*, no powers of the Height or of the Depth, *nor anything else in all creation* will be able to part us from God's love in Christ Jesus our Lord".[1] In the Christian faith of God's redeeming power and healing reconciliation it is implied that not man but God has taken and takes the first responsibility for setting the world right.

A theology of the laity has real meaning only if it is a normal part of the Church's view and work to recognize the laity's essential place and responsible partnership in the Church's vocation, and so to enable them to *stand* in the faith and to constitute an adult Christianity, a fraternal Christocracy, in which the weak and the strong, the simple and the educated, the influential and the common are nevertheless directed by one spirit and purpose, to be a real community in Christ, showing real signs of redemption, of a life free from the destructive self-centredness which enslaves man. For this is the meaning of redemption, and the world yearns, knowingly or unknowingly, for signs of redemption. In other words: "for the manifestation of the Sons of God" (Rom. 8:19).

It is deeply impressive that a writer like Albert Camus in his latest novel, *La Chute*,[2] gives such deep expression to the enslavement to self-centredness as the besetting sin, also or perhaps rather in men who consciously want to act nobly. An expression vivid and to the quick, such as one seldom meets in any "Christian" book. It is the more expressive because Camus takes it for granted that God is out of date and,

[1] Moffatt's translation. The italicized words are at present particularly relevant.　[2] E. T. *The Fall*, 1957.

although his intention in depicting his "hero" is virtually a passionate cry for redemption, he is convinced that the world is unredeemed and unredeemable, because he himself has decided for the blind universe.

Equally impressive is Martin Buber's argument, which he has hurled in the face of the Christian world; viz. the affirmation that in Jesus the Messiah (the Redeemer) has come cannot be true. Else the world would not look so utterly unredeemed. The Jewish expectation of the Messiah still to come is therefore more trustworthy.

It is better not to argue about these two trenchant utterances on redemption. The principal point is that true signs of redemption are legitimately expected from the Church, whose main message is about the Redeemer and the community of the redeemed.

A LAY THEOLOGY—OBEDIENCE AND GRATITUDE

There is a famous distinction between "theologia crucis" and "theologia gloriae". It is particularly beloved in some regions of continental Europe, under the influence of Martin Luther. It has a deep meaning, wanting to remind Christians that we are living as an "ekklèsia militans", under the Cross, in the period of toil and suffering. Not as an "ekklèsia triumphans". It seems that an ecclesiology of which a theology of the laity is an essential and organic part has little propensity towards a "theologia gloriae", because the organic incorporation of the laity in the self-understanding of the Church is a hindrance to presenting the Church as a glorious abstraction from ordinary reality. The theology which the Bible suggests as a background of a theology of the laity is a "theologiae obedientiae et gratitudinis", a theology of obedience and gratitude. The Church, if she knows what she is, viz. Christ's special domain, cannot take her orientation from the revolutionary state of our time. She watches and discerns "the signs of the times", but these are not her directives. Her directive is Christ, the Lord's authority and the obedience to Him. There is a remarkable passage in Peter's address to the Sanhedrin (Acts 5:32): "To these facts (i.e. the resurrection, ascension and work of salvation of Jesus) we bear witness *with the Holy Spirit*, which God has given to those *who obey* Him". Not our traditions, nor our historical antecedents, have the right to be the first directives in our thinking on the Church and its meaning, but the Lordship of Christ as an ever actual and active relation. If not, then it is forgotten that the reason of the Church's existence is not its continual self-affirmation and self-assertion, but its ministry to the Gospel and the world. Only by living in vigilant obedience, open to the urgings of its Lord and the Holy Spirit, can it in our modern world be a witness whose apostolate is believable, because this obedience means the readiness to evangelize itself while evangelizing the world.

But this obedience is joyful obedience. An obedience to God, to Jesus Christ the Lord, which is not joyful, is a contradiction. For this obedience is the response to God's redeeming and saving acts. Therefore a doctrine of the Church has to be in essence a declaration of grateful obedience, a pronouncement of obedient, grateful allegiance. In 1 Thess. 5:18 Paul says: "In every thing give thanks, for this is the will of God in Christ Jesus concerning you." The striking argumentation: "for this (to thank, to be grateful *in*, not *for* everything) is the *will* of God in *Christ Jesus* concerning you" shows that this passage is not a simple exhortation, one of the many the Apostle gives for the guidance of religious and moral conduct in the Christian way. It evidently represents a very fundamental consideration. We are called to give thanks in everything, not as an act of Christian religious and moral heroism or athletics, but as an act of obedience to God's will in Jesus Christ. This fundamental consideration becomes clear in the light of Rom. 1:21. The natural relation between God and men is that of thankfulness, of never forgetting Him as the source of all Good. Paul expresses this negatively by saying in Rom. 1:21: "Though they knew God, they have not glorified Him as God nor given thanks to him." This forgetting of the glorification of God and of thankfulness to Him, this deviation from the right relation between God and man, is the basic cause of all other deviations in human life. Therefore "to give thanks in everything" is "the will of God in Jesus Christ concerning us".

Along these lines it is possible to maintain that ecclesiology is an aspect of Christology, that the Church is a community in participation with Christ and living in grateful obedience to Him. In a Church so conceived, the laity has its natural and necessary place. The whole matter of what is often treated under the heading of *notae ecclesiae* (marks of the Church) then gets a different orientation, because the *primacy* of obedience to Christ and the Holy Spirit, which has its full validity at every moment of history, dissolves the rigidity which in our existing doctrines of the Church is often so striking. They give a static structure to a body which is by its nature and calling dynamic. The

real *notae ecclesiae* or marks of the Church must therefore in the first place express this dynamic character.
Let us venture a few risky observations in this field.

RECOGNIZING THE CHURCH

One of the astounding things in the present ecumenical discussion on the ecclesiological problem is
the statement often heard, particularly from the side
of what is commonly called the "catholic" branch,
that large parts of the Church have never developed a
full-sized ecclesiology. Strictly theologically speaking
there is truth in this statement, because in the Western
world the great schism of the Reformation forced men
to give more specific attention to the doctrine of the
Church as a special theological subject. Just as the
Ecumenical Movement to-day stimulates this thinking
again. But in fact the situation is quite different.
There have been in all Churches from the beginning
very influential patterns of self-understanding and self-
examination which have found their expression in
differing views on the *notae ecclesiae*, and conflicting
pretensions as to where the true and authentic Church
is to be found. In most cases, it seems, this trend of
development has historic justifications which it would
be unwise to disregard. Yet, as it seems to me, it cannot
be denied that it has also contributed to a self-centredness and self-affirmation, which weaken the extravert
character which in the context of God's design, with
His Church and with the world, is peculiar to it.

The "notae" which are universally accepted are the
two Sacraments: Baptism and the Eucharist, and the
Word. Especially in the Churches of the Reformation
are they prominent because over against Rome, which

had corrupted and obscured the Word and corrupted the Eucharist, the "evangelium recte docetur et Sacramenta recte administrantur"[1] were strongly stressed as the essential marks of the "congregatio sanctorum seu fidelium".[2] Nobody will even dream of denying the overwhelming importance of the interpretation of the Word of God as one of the bases of the Church and of the Sacraments. Especially should the latter be far more the living centres in the Church's regular worship and community life than they really are and should be expected to be by the crucial value accorded them. Liturgical movements, which try to recover just that for the Church, are real contributions to the renewal of the Church and the deepening of its life. Also is it true that the Church is recognizable in all distinctness by the Word and the Sacraments. From the beginning of the Church with Pentecost the inspired preaching of the word, Baptism as entrance into the fellowship, and the partaking in the Lord's Meal have been the inseparable and indispensable badges and nourishers of the Church. The building-up of the Church (Paul calls it *oikodomè*) takes place through the various forms of common worship.

Yet one wonders whether, especially in our day, it is adequate to stress them so exclusively as the essential marks of the Church. This is not said to minimize them. Rather to give them fuller scope in a wider vision of the being and calling of the Church. It is said, because the stress on their being the foremost and essential marks of the Church suggests over-strongly that the Church is a cultic community. Again, however

[1] "The Gospel rightly taught and the Sacraments rightly administered."
[2] "Congregation of the saints or of the faithful."

much it is true that cult, worship, belongs to the core of the Church, its calling is to be a "spiritual house of living stones", proclaiming God's wondrous deeds, being "a new creation" in the midst of the old creation, a body under marching orders. The concentration on considerations of rights and validity, on ordinances and the observance of rites, on the different theological accounts of the mystery hidden in the Lord's Meal as the appropriation of His atoning death, has done more in the course of history to conceal and obscure the Church than to manifest its true nature. A great many of the laity look at such things with a far greater lack of interest than often is realized. Moreover, the predominant concentration on these marks of the Church as the only essential ones has contributed enormously to the feeling amongst the laity of being objects and not subjects in the Church. It artificially narrows our thinking on the Church, its being and purpose. It is the reason why the ecumenical discussion on the Church continues to centre around Ministry and Sacraments. This is too narrow. For a more untrammelled manifestation of the true nature and calling of the Church it is essential to grasp the point that the laity is as truly and fully subject in the Church as the ministry and clergy are.

The self-understanding of the Church which we need is one which shows the evidence of this view on biblical grounds. Not because a biblical self-understanding of the Church should intend to repristinate the forms and patterns in the New Testament. There is not one form and pattern there, but a plurality of them, so that different ecclesiologies can pretend to substantiate their claims by fixing too exclusively on isolated passages. Biblical self-understanding means to seize the dominant intention and to grasp the motives, the power and spirit, by which the Church is *moved* and in which it has its real being. Karl Barth expresses this clearly and vigorously in his words: " Der heilige Geist ist die belebende Macht, in der Jesus der Herr, die Christenheit in der Welt auferbaut als seinen Leib d.h. als seine eigene irdisch-geschichtliche Existenzform, sie wachsen läszt, erhält und ordnet als die Gemeinschaft seiner Heiligen und so tauglich macht zur vorläufigen Darstellung der in ihm geschehenen Heiligung der ganzen Menschenwelt."[1]

The Holy Spirit has generated the Church. It is the work of the Holy Spirit. This appears quite plainly in the story of Pentecost. Therefore, the Church cannot dispose of the Holy Spirit or of Christ and what He has done. Christ and the Holy Spirit are the true Disposers of the Church. Christ is the Lord and He it is who has the Holy Spirit and sends Him. Not the Church, whose characteristic it is to pray for and expect the Holy Spirit, confessing thereby its true dependence on God, the Father, the Son and the Holy Spirit. It is just this dependence as the true, vivifying source of its life which marks it off from the rest of the world as a peculiar body. The Church did not enter the world as an institution, but as a community expecting the Kingdom of God. It *became* an institution, but is as such only truly legitimate in so far as it serves this end.

[1] " The Holy Spirit is the animating force whereby Jesus, the Lord, builds up Christianity in the world as His Body, that is, as His own historical form of existence on earth; lets it grow, preserves and orders it as the community of His saints and so makes it fit to be the preliminary representation of the sanctifying of the whole human world that took place through Him." *Church Dogmatics* IV/2, p. 695 in German edition.

Chapter 5

A THEOLOGY OF THE LAITY

I N justice to the whole account of the history of God's
self-disclosure, aiming at the salvation and redemption of the world, it must be stated as a first point
that God is concerned about the world. In all that has
happened in Christ, the whole of mankind is in God's
view. The Church is provisional, not definitive. Consequently, the Church does not primarily exist on
behalf of itself, but on behalf of the world. Strange to
say, this elementary truth, which finds ready intellectual
assent, is nevertheless absent in the Church. Even the
deeper feeling of evangelistic responsibility and the
many kinds of work which are done by the Churches
as a contribution to the general need of society do not
change the striking fact that the Church as such is introvert, and considered as such by public opinion. It has
been bred for centuries into the Church and therefore it
is felt as natural by Church people themselves and by
public opinion. The enormous amount of time that is
spent in self-glorification of the Churches, the extent to
which it has often sacralized itself, are indications of
this. Without entering into a discussion of the many
reasons, good and bad, valid and invalid, which have
caused this situation, the upshot of it is that the mind of
the Churches is bent, above all, on its own increase and
well-being. It is Church-centred. It is self-centred.
The interest in the world is at best a side-issue. The
concern, one may even say the burning concern about
the world and its needs, which fills the Bible, which is

the impelling power behind that whole history of God's self-disclosure, does not find a real reflection in the "normal" attitude of the "normal" Churches and in the attitude of its "normal" members.

And yet, this all-pervading concern about the world in need, about the world in its lostness (even in its great achievements and triumphs) is basic to the true meaning of the Church. As the salt pervades all the waters of the ocean, so this eager, interested concern for the world should pervade the Church in all its manifestations. As an imitation of God, an imitation of Christ. A few crucial moments in the drama of God's concern about the lost world, which is nevertheless His world, may be mentioned.

After, in the first chapters of Genesis, the fateful parting of ways between God and Man has been told, God's resolve to "pursue" man in his unfolding history appears frequently. The so-called Noachite Covenant (Chapter 9) is a covenant which God is shown as proposing between Himself and "every living creature of all flesh that is upon the earth". With Abraham God begins that movement of contraction, of concentration, which makes Israel His elect people and chosen instrument of His special revelation. This contraction, which might be an arbitrary act of unmotivated predilection, offensive to reason and justice, has, however, the same nature and function as the contraction of the human heart. That is to say: the heart contracts in order that the bloodstream may fill, vivify and serve the whole body. God singles out for a universal purpose. Abram is told to leave his own country and family in blind faith to go to an unknown land in order to become the father of a great nation. But the final word about this elective and selective act of God is: "in thee shall

all families of the earth be blessed". In choosing Israel, God holds fast to His purpose with the world.

The prophets were the faithful interpreters of this divine concern, which is the primary reason for the existence of the Christian Church. John 3:16 says clearly that God so loved the *world* that he gave His only begotten Son. It is not said that he so loved the faithful, the believers, the Church. The world is His purpose. Jesus in His prayer: "Thy will be done on earth as it is in heaven" sees the world as the theatre of God's activity. Paul in his manifold endeavours to interpret the infinitely deep and wide meaning of this great event, viz. Jesus Christ coming into the world, keeps to what Simeon said in his hymn (Luke 2: 29-32): "for mine eyes have seen thy saving power which thou hast prepared before the face of all the peoples, to be a light of revelation for the Gentiles and a glory to thy people Israel". One of the most telling is his weighty word in 2 Cor. 5: 19: "For in Christ God reconciled *the world* unto Himself". It shows deep insight in a great Christian like Dietrich Bonhoeffer that in his posthumous, fragmentary work on "Ethics" he takes the starting-point of Christian Ethics from this reconciliation of the world with God, and so can say that the problem of Christian Ethics is the real appearance of God's revelational reality in Christ amongst all His creatures.[1] We said before that the Church is provisional, not definitive. Paul opens up the wide scope of the redemption of Christ by putting it in the tremendous words of Eph. 1: 9, 10: God "has granted us complete insight and understanding of the open secret of His will, showing us how it was the purpose of his

[1] p. 57 in the German edition.

design so to order it in the fulness of the ages that all things in heaven and earth alike should be gathered up in Christ " (Moffatt).

THE CHURCH EXISTS FOR THE WORLD

So, on the ground of the inner meaning and scope of God's self-disclosing and saving dealing with the world as a whole, the Church, being called to the "imitation" of God and of Jesus Christ who is the Lord of the world and of the Church, should be always conscious of this basic fact that it primarily exists on behalf of the world and not of itself. That is its basic law of existence. It cannot be too often repeated and reminded, because history evidences a pernicious tendency to forget it. The great redemption through Christ, the "freedom of the children of God " in Him, consists in the liberation from self-regard and self-centredness which is the central sin and root of all corruption in human life. The appalling strength of this fundamental power in human life is verified in a sad way by the pernicious tendency in the Church to forget God's reaching out towards the world, for this forgetfulness is a falling back into self-regard and self-centredness. The Church by being *world-centred* in the image of the divine example, is really the Church. Being Church-centred, regarding the world of the Church as the safe refuge from the world, is a betrayal of its nature and calling. Only by not being or not wanting to be an end in itself, the Church arrives at being the Church.

Everybody who knows the world of the Churches as they are in empirical reality sees immediately that the opening sentences of this chapter, though so readily accepted and assented to, imply a radical reorientation in our ecclesiastical institutionalism and in the minds of its members. Radical means: from the roots (*radix*) upwards.

Starting from this fundamental orientation, the essential aspects of the Church as the body which Christ creates to Himself through the Holy Spirit are that the Church is missionary and ministerial. In these two aspects the being or the nature and the calling of the Church are expressed. It would merely engender a futile and hopeless discussion to propose these two aspects as the true *notae ecclesiae*. But one thing should be said. They belong to the Church as breathing to the human body. They direct the eyes of the Church and of its members continuously to its reason for existence and to the ground and creative force of its existence and subsistence: the Lord Jesus Christ and the Holy Spirit. They keep the Church away from all temptations to self-contemplation and self-extolment. They hold it within the bounds of being above all an instrument, a chosen vessel, for God's purposes.

THE CHURCH *IS* MISSION

To say that the Church is missionary or apostolic by nature and calling needs some closer consideration. A more adequate way of expressing this aspect is: the Church *is* Mission. This is something quite different from what is commonly meant when we speak about the missionary task or obligation of the Church. In the minds of people the missionary task or obligation of the Church is conceived as being one of its many activities. Perhaps one of its important and great activities, but at any rate an activity in regard to which one can take different attitudes, of real involvement or of greater or lesser detachment. This possibility, which is in ordinary Church life a reality, contradicts the nature and calling of the Church, if it is true that the Church *is* Mission, and not only *has* Missions as one form˙ of its activities. The Church *has* Missions suggests that there are certain times and certain parts of the world in and on which this activity becomes an actual fact. The Church *is* Mission implies that it is in all times and places the world-wide and local-near embrace of the world, in and to which it is sent.

Why should we say : the Church *is* Mission, of which the phrase: the Church *has* Missions is only a derivative? It is implied in all that we have stated about God's concern for the whole of mankind. It transpires, however, very clearly in various passages of the Bible. It has always been the custom to motivate the missionary activity of the Church with the Great Commandment: "Go ye therefore and teach all nations, baptizing them in the name of the Father and the Son and the Holy Spirit, and teach them to obey all the things whatsoever I have commanded you, and lo, I am with you always unto the end of the world." It is the will of the Lord, and it is an unending task. If the missionary expansion of the Church were, however, only the fulfilling of an obligation, then Mission would be a "mark" of the Church, but not its very essence. Acts 1:8 goes deeper. "Ye shall receive power after that the Holy Spirit is come upon you and ye shall be witnesses unto me . . . unto the end of the earth." The Holy Spirit is the Baptizer of the Church into witness-bearing. When Jesus has His intimate meetings with His disciples, which must have been of great significance to them and of which we know so little, there is in John 20:21 recorded a word of great profundity: "Peace be with you! As the Father has sent me, even so I send you." The disciples become apostles. Jesus Christ is the Apostle (John 17:3) *kat' exochèn*. The inner urge of God towards the world entered into the world in Jesus Christ, and through the Church this divine urge continues. The Church is the community of the "sent", just as she is the community of the witnesses. She is sent to and into the world.

The whole Bible is filled with divine calling and sending. Therefore it is said that the Church is built on the foundation of prophets and apostles. The oneness, the unity of the Church and Mission (Apostolate) are organically connected. From a psychological point of view this relation between Mission and Unity seems very convincing or at any rate persuasive. In a Church which is above all bent on its Mission and so develops its Kerygma in encounter with the world, out of concern to be a true witness, divergences and quarrels do not arise easily, leading in a pernicious way towards forgetting the brotherhood and the bond of charity. In this same line of thinking it is appropriate to say that in a world of ecclesiastical disruption one of the best ways for separated churches to learn the experience of sadness and shame about the scandal and riddle of disruption and separation, is to be put to the yoke of joint evangelism and Mission. Because then one feels more sharply than through any theological discussion that the bond of unity is in Christ and in Him alone, not in our synthetic formulas and compromises. Because in preaching that only in Him is there salvation it is better realized that it is not biblical doctrine to say: "extra ecclesiam nulla salus" (outside the Church there is no salvation), but: "extra Christum (outside Christ) nulla salus."

But however much truth these psychological, purely human considerations may contain, the oneness of Unity and Mission has deeper grounds. The true ecumenical question is not: how can we restore unity, but: is Christ divided? The absurdity of this last question is the best eye-opener for the intrinsic absurdity of schism, notwithstanding the many human and historical arguments that can be summoned to explain the absurdity. In John 17 at three places (vs. 18, 21 and 23) Jesus in His solemnizing prayer for His disciples keeps Unity and Mission in an indissoluble bond together. Vs. 18: "As thou hast sent me into the world, even so have I also sent them into the world." These words convey what might be called the divine apostolic succession. Because God is apostolic in sending His Son as His Apostle, the Church of this divine, unique Apostle is as a whole necessarily apostolic. This divine apostolic succession precedes and relativizes our conceptions of apostolic succession, whether taken in the sense of the only valid transmission of spiritual and even juridical authority and of sacramental power, or in that of keeping in continuity with the Church of all ages to the Apostles' doctrine. After having touched upon the fruits of this apostolic commission ("I pray for them also which shall believe on me through their word"), the oneness of Unity and Mission as inherent in the essential nature of the Church appears in vs. 21: "That they also may be one in us, *that the world may believe that thou hast sent me*." This is repeated in vs. 22, 23: "that they may be one even as we are one, I in them and thou in me, that

134

they may be made perfectly one so that the world may recognize *that thou hast sent me.*"

The only *fully* legitimate Mission is the Mission of the one Church. Missions as they have been happening since the 18th century up to now, grateful as we must be for them, are crippled, amputated Missions. The Unity or Oneness of the Church is the legitimation of Christ's and the Church's apostolate. The missionary or apostolic aspect expresses as well the being as the calling of the Church. This applies to the whole Church, to *all* its members. All members have this stamp and should acknowledge it with heart and mind. This has to stand as a basic affirmation and basic orientation of the Church. "All the members" for whom this is indicative as well as imperative, means to say that "ministry" or "clergy" and laity are equally implied. The particular emphasis upon the laity as the proper missionary body of the Church, which in all present writing on the laity is customary, is understandable and justified from the angle of the history of the Church, in which the laity has been so perseveringly ignored.[1] It is understandable too in our present situation, because it is not exaggeration to say that in the last decades the laity as an essential part of the Church, especially also in the discharge of its task, is a new discovery. This explains why the missionary calling of the laity is figuring so largely in the ever-increasing literature on the laity. From the standpoint of thinking on the meaning of the Church, however, it should be kept in mind that this missionary or apostolic stamp regards the total membership of the Church, and consequently the laity.

[1] Cf. Chapters 1 and 2.

THE CHURCH *IS* MINISTRY

It is a sign of our time that this manner of approach, compared with the preceding centuries, is new. Not only are the laity as a very relevant part of the Church, in the expression of its life and execution of its task, a new discovery. The missionary vocation of the laity, conceived in the resolute and outspoken way it is more and more proclaimed everywhere in the world of the Churches, is not less a new discovery. But, holding fast to this new discovery, we must soberly realize that the hardest days are ahead of us. It is one thing to see and seize it, another thing to give it shape and form in the reality of the Church and to weave it as the basic pattern in the lives of the laity, with their endless variety of gifts, abilities and natural endowments or lack of endowments. For the Church this means a readiness to revise its total outlook and its structure. For "ministry" and laity it means a laborious adventure of learning new lessons and finding new ways. In the process of finding them (and many encouraging things are already happening, as has been shown) and in finding them, it may become true that a laity, reborn to its true status and calling in the Church and in the world, will appear to be one of the main expressions of the Church's missionary being and calling,[1] the greatest potential it possesses. A greater and deeper-cutting potential than evangelistic "campaigns" and "crusades".

As the other essential aspect of the Church which Christ creates to Himself through the Holy Spirit, we mentioned the ministerial. The thesis that is also in

[1] These remarks on the "new discovery" of the laity are only preliminary. We will return later to this point.

this case put at the beginning, is that the Church, well understood, not so much *has* a ministry or ministries, but primarily *is* ministry. Of course it is true that the Church has a ministry and has ministries. Especially in our rapidly changing society the number of ministries is constantly increasing in number and changing in character, and rightly so. But this adaptability of the Church to changing patterns of life, in which is also included an increasing use of the term "the ministry of the laity", does not necessarily imply a new orientation. Our purpose is to express a new orientation in the brief phrase: the Church *is* ministry, and therefore *has* ministries. On the same level with the phrase: the Church *is* Mission, and therefore *has* Missions. But in both cases the priority of the "is" over the "has" engenders as result a new approach to the "missions" and the "ministries", both in the plural. Both: the Church *is* Mission; the Church *is* Ministry, as the first things to be said, have an intimate interdependence and interrelation. The essential missionary and apostolic aspect of the Church is as such also ministerial. It is a ministering to and in the world by the supremely necessary act: the proclaiming of Christ, the Truth, the Life, the Way, in word and deed. The essential ministerial aspect of the Church is as such also missionary, apostolic. All ministry is a witness to Christ, an overt or covert invitation to accept Him as the Lord of all life and each individual life. Why does it seem worthwhile and justified to say: the Church *is* Ministry and therefore *has* ministries?[1]

[1] This published edition of the Hulsean Lectures is a somewhat more elaborated account of what was in substance spoken in the Lectures. I will put here as a footnote some remarks which in the spoken Lectures had their place in the text.

I am deeply aware that to speak as a non-English lay theologian

For two main reasons: because of the evidence which shines through the New Testament in the centrality of the diakonia (ministry), and because of the Church's whole relation to Christ. The former is dependent on the latter. In taking a look at what transpires of the life of the primitive Church and the ordering of this life, it is indeed striking how prominent the word "ministry" or diakonia is. It is legitimate to take mainly, apart from the Acts, some of the Pauline Epistles as sources, because there this life appears in the most concrete terms. It appears less in the Acts, because this first little History of the Church is above all interested in the facts and the stir they made. Some of Paul's Epistles are real combats of the Apostle with the congregations, of which he himself was the spiritual father.

THE PRIMITIVE DIAKONIA

In its original sense diakonia simply means to act as a waiter at table; cf. for instance in the Gospels Luke 17:8. Jesus has made this simple word with its

in the famous and ancient University of Cambridge before a theological faculty, consisting of great scholars, about the Ministry of the Church is a very risky thing indeed. Perhaps it is too audacious. I am also deeply aware of the fact that England has produced more theologians than any other country, who have written extremely able books on the Ministry of the Church. By its history and by its comprehensive bias the Ministry naturally must be a central and crucial point in the Anglican approach to the problem of the Church. I want to confess frankly that, although I hope to have some understanding of the Anglican way of looking at it, I know only a very small fraction of the output of English books on the subject. Therefore one will not hear me quote for example (to mention only two famous names on the subject) Gore or Moberly and a great deal of other very important English literature.

humble origin the typical expression for the spirit and relationships within the community of His disciples. It indicates in a drastic way the re-evaluation of all value-scales which Jesus in His person, His work and His words, as we will see, has introduced into the world of human relationships. The totality of life is put under the principle of diakonia, of which "ministry" is the usual translation, but which, to avoid the associations which have grown up around the word "ministry" in its secular and religious meanings, could perhaps be better translated by "servantship". In Peter's Epistle[1] it is expressed very succinctly as a basic law for the life of Christians and of a Christian congregation: "You must serve one another, each with the talent (*charisma*) he has received as efficient stewards (*oikonomoi*) of God's varied grace" (Moffatt). From the preceding verses it appears that the root of this attitude of service is love; from what follows, that this diakonia manifests itself in word and deed. In Revelation 2:19 in the list of the good points of the "Church" of Thyatira we find amongst love and faith and endurance especial mention of diakonia.

In the primitive Church every activity or function which contributed to the upbuilding of the Christian community was brought under the category of diakonia. All Christians are *diakonoi*, ministers, called to a ministry. A particularly important passage is Eph. 4:11, 12, which gets the more weight because from the whole context it is evident that it all manifests the essential oneness and wholeness of the Church. "And He gave some to be apostles, some to be prophets, some to be evangelists and some as shepherds and

[1] 1 Peter 4:10.

teachers, for the equipment of the saints for the work of diakonia, for the upbuilding of the body of Christ." The last sentence is of peculiar importance. The customary way to read it has always been to separate " the equipment of the saints" by a comma from "for the work of diakonia", because diakonia was translated by " ministry", conceived in the sense of a special category of people with a special function, " the ministry". W. Robinson[1] is quite right in maintaining that the Greek text does not give any support to putting a comma after "saints". It is really startling to notice how radically the meaning of the text is altered by the removal of this comma. It restores to the text the meaning which fits in with the picture the New Testament gives of *all* the saints, i.e. all the members, being ministers, servants to the upbuilding of the Church. It rules out the use of the text as a corroboration for the condition of the Church as we know it by tradition, viz. the " ministry", the diakonia as a specialized sphere. Of this specialized sphere the Church in its primitive, fluid state was scarcely conscious. All the stress was on the diakonia, the ministry of the whole membership, because the Church as a whole stood under the same token as its Lord, i.e. " servantship".

The Twelve showed that they had understood the mind of their Master, because they saw the Apostolate itself under the category of diakonia (Acts 1 : 17). In 1 Cor. 12 : 4-30 Paul speaks about all the work, the manifestations of spiritual power and gifts as " varieties of diakonia". His own work and that of his co-workers is a " ministry of reconciliation"; they are *diakonoi* (servants) of the New Covenant, or *diakonoi*

[1] *Op. cit.,* p. 21.

of Christ. Notwithstanding his extraordinarily strong personality and his deep conviction that he is an apostle "by the will of God"; in spite of the commanding position he could claim in many a congregation, of which he was the founder and leader, Paul was in such a deep sense a prisoner of Christ and His Spirit that he never really claimed authority to which one had to submit. It is rather in the second Epistle to the Corinthians, just that Epistle which is so full of plain, human excitement and argument with his flock, that he states (1:24): "Not that we have lordship over your faith, but are helpers of your joy, for by faith ye stand." Paul shows here a deep awareness of who the *kurios* is, whose servant, whose slave (*doulos*) he simply is, and therefore also a deep recognition of the independence of the Christians, his converts, from him, because he and they were jointly dependent on the common Lord. The expression "helpers of your joy", i.e. co-operator in your joy, is another way of saying what diakonia means. In his Epistles, which deal with so many difficulties and problems, he always pleads that all the members should be constantly mindful that, whatever gifts they have, they have been given for the "common good" in order that all the members may have the same care for one another (1 Cor. 12:7, 25). It is this spirit of mutual diakonia which is the antidote to schism. More than once Paul reminds the Christians that he himself has always tried in his intercourse with them to give them an example, to honour by his conduct the concern for "the common good" (2 Thess. 3:7-9).

The so-called "Pastoral Epistles" to Timothy and Titus, which reflect already a less fluid state of affairs in the primitive Churches and show signs of the institution of "office-bearers", not merely of charismatic vocations and functions, nevertheless continue freely to speak in the terms and the true spirit of diakonia. Timothy's whole work, Paul's work also remains essentially diakonia.

Women as well as men were considered *diakonoi*, ministers, because women by being called to be " saints " (i.e. members of the Church) were just as men equally called to serve God's purpose in the world. There were outstanding women amongst them (Acts 18:26, 21:9. Rom. 16:1, 3, 4, 12). The later, exclusively male development of the functioning of the Church, interspersed with interesting timid endeavours to reserve some place for certain categories of women in the Church's official service, represents an estrangement from the dominant thought of the New Testament that the *whole* Church, regardless of sex, *is* diakonia (ministry).

An abiding testimony to the pre-eminent place of diakonia in the total outlook and attitude of the new community in Christ, is to the present day the habit of calling the whole body of ordained office-bearers the ministry. It certainly does not square with the fact that within the structure of most Churches the *diakonos* (deacon), the diakonia, has become a subordinate function. The need for emphasizing in all functions the fundamental importance of its ultimately " ministerial " character has often exercised and is exercising a wholesome influence, but it has not that dynamic and all-regulative place which pervades the New Testament. A recovery of the true meaning of the ministerial nature of the Church, not only in the sense of activity but of being, would entail a careful scrutiny of the inherent tendency of our Church structures towards a division of authorities and powers instead of a radically Christ-centred diakonia. The basic fact that the Church *is* ministry (diakonia), because it is correlative to and rooted in Christ's ministry (diakonia), has to enter into full vigour again.[1] The ministry of the ordained clergy and the ministry of the laity are both aspects of the same diakonia, each in their proper sphere and calling.

THE CHURCH *IS* DIAKONIA

This leads us to the real basis of our point: the Church *is* Ministry. It has already become clear that in using this term we must constantly make a desperate effort to free ourselves from most of the suggestions and associations, which during many centuries have grown in ecclesiastical use around the word ministry. It is therefore better to say: the Church *is* diakonia. Because Christ Himself placed diakonia in the centre of understanding the meaning of His person and work. This intimate relation between the Church's diakonia or ministry and Christ's is not an identity of both, because Christ's ministry or diakonia is unique, *sui generis*; but it is a participation in Christ's[2] ministry by *serving Him* and so each other and the world. In this lies the sole "honour" or "glory" of the Church. In nothing else. The often repeated rejections of "boasting" (*kauchèma*) by Paul issue from this conviction.

One of the attempts to define the relation between Christ and His Church has been the well-known doctrine of the *munus triplex*: Christ is Prophet, Priest and King, and the prophetic, priestly and kingly func-

[1] Cf. T. F. Torrance: *Royal Priesthood*, p. 35.
[2] Cf. T. F. Torrance, *op. cit.*

143

tions of the Church are a reflection of Christ's *munera*; to use Torrance's words, are correlatively prophetic, priestly and kingly. It has in many respects been a very helpful doctrine, because it gave a comprehensive picture of the great dimensions of manifestation of Christ's diakonia, Christ's ministry to the world. Especially in our time, in which the Church finds itself in the position of restating its meaning, this doctrine stands in various quarters in high favour. One can easily understand this favourable estimate, because this doctrine helps to define at the same time its independence of this world and its structures and powers and its solidarity with the world in the world's deepest needs and perplexities. Firm, unbridgeable distance and deep, truly committed involvement in one.

Nevertheless, although this doctrine has firm biblical roots, from a biblical point of view it is incomplete. It is taken too much for granted that the fulness of Christ and of the Church is expressed in these three great representative titles: Prophet, Priest, King. An indication of this incompleteness has already been hinted at in saying that all three are the expression of His being a *diakonos*. In the Gospels Jesus speaks as one who has authority, who is the fulfiller of the words of the Prophets, but He only by suggestion presents Himself as the Prophet *kat' exochèn*. The tersest and deepest expression of His—one might say—unique prophethood is that He *is* the Word (Logos) of God, that came into the world. This is essentially different from the position of the prophets, which was characterized by " the word of the Lord came to me "; " thus says the Lord ".

Jesus, although it is deeply true that He is the

true High Priest, never speaks in terms of priesthood about Himself. He speaks in terms of being *the* sacrifice, and at the same time by His willingness to be the sacrifice, carrying away the sins of the world, being the sacrificer, the Priest. When he refers to it, He does so in different terms; that is, in declaring Himself the Suffering Servant (*diakonos*). Also he only occasionally pointed to His kingship, particularly in His brief utterances before Pilate.

This does not in the least mean to say that the Gospels are reticent about the reality of Jesus' Prophethood, Priesthood or Kingship, leaving aside the outspoken emphasis put on it in all apostolic preaching. Nor am I forgetting the resurrection and the ascension, which are crucial to a full understanding of Christ's ministry or diakonia to the world; nor do I intend to ground the ministry, the diakonia, of the Church on the historical Jesus alone.[1] The point I want to make and which seems to me worthwhile to be made, is first that according to the record of the Gospels Jesus dwells, in comparison to prophethood, priesthood and kingship, comparatively speaking frequently and expressly on the fundamental significance of His being a *diakonos*, because of which one of the key-names of His disciples should also be *diakonos*. Second, that if one looks carefully at those passages, it appears that everything that has to be said about Christ the Prophet, the Priest and the King and about the Church as serving Him in these functions, gets its right setting in diakonia as *its proper frame of reference*. Both the frequent speaking about diakonia and its being proclaimed the fundamental law of the Church's existence and expression,

[1] T. F. Torrance, *op. cit.*, p. 36, is right in warning against such tendencies.

and of Christian existence altogether, are crucially important.

Matthew 20:25-28 lays down the law: " Whosoever will be chief among you, let him be your *diakonos*." " Whosoever will be first among you, must be your *doulos* (slave)." What is the argument for this imperative rule? The answer is vs. 28: " Just as the Son of Man has not come to be served, but to serve " (to be *diakonos*). This rule, which reflects His being and meaning, is formulated—and this is significant to note—to mark the real distance of the new dimension of the Church from the old dimension of the world. In the world, lust for power is the rule. "But it shall not be so among you." The lust for power and dominion is exchanged for lust for diakonia.[1] Jesus stipulates very definitely (Luke 22:27): " I am among you as a *diakonos*, a servant." In Phil. 2:7 Paul places the Incarnation in the light of emptying Himself of His divine eminence, becoming a *doulos*, a servant. This spirit of divine humility, which was in Jesus Christ, Paul recommends as the characteristic Christian spirit (vs. 5).

The most impressive testimony is found in John 13, the story of Jesus washing the feet of the disciples. Here Jesus not only speaks, but He acts symbolically. It is the more impressive, because according to universal opinion this story is the Johannine equivalent of the story of the Last Supper in the Synoptics. Jesus in explaining His misunderstood act to the disciples

[1] Cf. also Mark 9:35; Luke 22:25-27. The words, full of prophetical fervour, of Matthew 7:21 about the "Lord, Lord " sayers and the doing of God's will, and particularly Jesus' gripping picture of the Last Judgment in which the sole criterion will be what one has done in diakonia to His least ones, in Matthew 25:31-46, undoubtedly belong to the theme of diakonia.

first states firmly that they do well in calling Him Lord and Master, but ends up by saying: the servant is not more than his Lord. So if diakonia is the all-pervading motivation of Christ's meaning for the world, of all that He has done, it is *a fortiori* the reason of existence of the Church, the only proper way to be His *diakonos*, to serve Him.

This whole matter gets a still deeper meaning if we keep in mind that the decisive moment in Jesus' earthly existence was the moment when after much groping and struggling He saw the awful truth that He was meant by His Father to be the Suffering Servant, the living and revealing commentary on Isaiah 53.[1] In being *so*, He is the Prophet, the Priest and the King.[2]

DIAKONIA—ROOTED IN THE PERSON OF CHRIST

Our conclusion is therefore that diakonia as the true spirit and pattern of the Church has its root in the being and the work of Jesus Christ her Lord Himself.

[1] Cf. T. F. Torrance, pp. 82 ff., where I find when writing down these lectures, to my delight, a more elaborate theological treatment of this same line of thought than I intend to give, p. 87: " It is indeed in terms of the suffering-servant ministry that we are to see the basic unity in the Church's prophetic, priestly and kingly functions ". For several years it has formed a main point of my thinking on the subject.

[2] In finishing our observations on the centrality of diakonia in the interpretation of Christ and of the Church as Ministry, we cannot refrain from remarking that this has also consequences for our doctrine of God. To say the least, it invites to a critical revision of our usual treatment of the so-called attributes of God. Christ is the revealer of God's heart, and in being the humble and suffering Servant (" I am gentle and humble in heart " Matthew 11:29) He discloses the awe-inspiring (perhaps often also the offensive) truth that the God and Father of Jesus Christ is, in all his unapproachable Holy Majesty, humble and *diakonos*.

It is not merely the following of an ethical example, but a living in a new, divinely created order of existence. The religious and ethical are distinct and yet inseparably one in this new world in Christ, of which the Church is the proclaimer and is called to be the demonstrator. Proclamation and demonstration are of the greatest importance for the Church's participation in the world and all its concerns, which is the tremendous task she has to face at present and in which the significance of the laity cannot be easily over-estimated. It is rather easy to formulate this view of the Church in the light of diakonia as a theological proposition. It is even possible to see and seize it as irrefutable truth about and for the Church, for its being and for its calling. But again in this case, as in that of the apostolic essence of the Church, it is one thing to see and seize it as a fascinating theme of theological speculation. It is another thing to translate it into terms of life and reality, which testify to the prime reality that the Church, if it understands itself rightly, is planted and participating in the ministry, the diakonia to the world, of Jesus Christ, the *Suffering Diakonos*.

We must be realistic therefore and combine affirmations of the true, creative reality of the Church with sober constatations of the disturbing *obliviousness* to this basic reality, which has the Church so often in its grip. The diakonia, the "servantship", is infinite, even as the world of "neighbours" and needs and interests is infinite. The point in the Parable of the Good Samaritan is that the answer to the question: Who is my neighbour? is not an attempt to find an all-comprehensive definition, but that Jesus in fact says to the Scribe: Stop asking the question: Who is my neighbour? You yourself are always the neighbour.

Here it becomes very evident that the laity, living in the world as an integral part of it, is the primary body, through which the reality of the phrase: the Church *is* diakonia, *is* Ministry, has to be manifested in all spheres of secular life. The "world-diakonia" of the Church, which has entered into the ecumenical realm of discussion and action, can only be truly preserved from the danger of becoming either a humanitarian action with some Christian colouring, or a camouflaged form of Missions,[1] if it has its basic motivation and its inspiration in this view of Christ the *Diakonos*, in whom all diakonia as response to His diakonia is at the same time a religious confession and an act of specific ethical quality.

Christ, the *Diakonos*, the Servant, is the Lord. The Lord of and in the Church. The Lord of the world. Through Christ's diakonia as it happened and happens through His life, His teaching, His death, His resurrection, God's redemptive order is established and active in the world. Again, the *is* here is essential. Redemption means liberation from slavery (*douleia*), the liberation from the slavery of sin. For the Bible does not see sin only as a hidden conflict with God by falling out of His obedience, but also as a slavery to a foreign illegitimate power. Redemption means also, therefore, liberation from these "powers", these usurpers of God's place of Lordship, by which man in his individual and collective social, political, economic and cultural life is enslaved. The Church *being* Ministry, *being* diakonia in correlation to Christ's diakonia or Ministry, has the imperative calling to show in her own life signs and evidences of this redemptive

[1] At any rate, the non-Christians will interpret it in that way.

divine order which is in Christ an operative fact. When we speak in one breath about Jesus the Servant, the *Diakonos*, and Jesus the Lord, it should never be forgotten (how often it has!) that Christ's Kingship in this dispensation is a *hidden* Kingship, hidden in His "Servant"-ship. He is the King reigning from the Cross, in the depth of humiliation. He is not yet the King of Glory. The world can only experience the reality of this hidden Kingship and of the operating redemptive order in Christ according to the measure of the faith, the hope, the love, the courage and the endurance, which live in the Church.

The conclusion to which we have to come for the moment is that the famous doctrine of the *munus triplex* (prophet, priest and king) needs a very important modification in the way it is used and presented. This can be expressed by saying that it has to be deepened and widened into a *munus quadruplex*: diakonos, prophet, priest, king. Or by saying that the hallowed offices of prophet, priest and king get their right perspective and meaning (to use the words already quoted from Torrance) only in "the suffering-servant ministry".

There is, however, still another incompleteness in the *munus triplex* doctrine. One of the central dimensions in biblical thinking is the "pastoral" one. In the Old Testament the relation of rulers and their peoples is put in the light of that of shepherds (pastors) and flock. Amongst all the great ancient peoples of the Orient it was a beloved form of speech.[1] It is

---

[1] Homer speaks about the king as *poimèn laou*, the shepherd of the people. This universality of the symbol is not an argument against its special significance in the Bible. Priest and king are also universal terms.

presented in the Old Testament, not as a beautiful figure of speech, nor properly speaking as an ideal pattern for kings and rulers, but as the relation which is God's will and, therefore, an indispensable mark of the divine order of human existence.[1] A particularly eloquent passage is to be found in Ezekiel 34:1-16. This and other passages in other prophets show that the righteousness which exalts rulers and nations reflects divine righteousness only if it is pervaded by mercifulness. Our current use of the shepherd symbol is too exclusively influenced by the individualistic use of the famous Psalm 23. Frequently in the Old Testament God is called the Shepherd of His flock, the people of Israel. The many passages in the New Testament are well known. Jesus presents in the parable of the lost sheep, in Luke 15:4-6, God as the Shepherd. He presents Himself as the Shepherd, who defends His sheep with His life (John 10). In John 10 also, He not only stresses the burning concern He has for the lost, the erring and the despised, but pictures His view of the future of His community in the words: "There shall be one fold and one Shepherd." In John 21, Peter is expressly confirmed as shepherd. Looking at the multitude He is moved with compassion because they were shepherdless sheep. When reading the passage in Nazareth's synagogue from Isaiah 61 about the brokenhearted and the bruised, He adds, to the astonishment of the hearers, the remark: "This day is this Scripture fulfilled in your ears" (Luke 4).

These few examples must suffice for our purpose.[2]

[1] Plato expresses a kindred idea. Cf. Kittel's *Wörterbuch*, under *poimèn*.

[2] In this case also we do not pretend to offer a full exegetical and systematic study of this aspect as part of an attempt at a theology of the laity.

In the Acts (20:28) and in the Epistles (e.g. Eph. 4:11; I Peter 5:2) the word "shepherd" is used for the responsible leaders of the Christian congregations. To the present day it has been the custom in all churches to call those who have the care of the congregation as their specific work, shepherds, pastors. Just as "minister", the term "pastor" is known and widely used for the leading office-bearers in the Churches. In that respect Christendom has not been at all oblivious of the eminence of the term "shepherd". In the many books on the Ministry in the current sense of the word, and on the implications of pastoral care, the Christian Churches have always shown a great awareness of the implications of its pastoral obligation. Yet this great awareness has never found expression in the conscious expression of the being and calling of Christ and the correlative being and calling of the Church. It is, although the pastoral aspect is fundamentally speaking a variation of the ministerial, part of the diakonia, it has its own relevancy and tone. It helps greatly to get some idea of the fulness of Christ in His all-embracing compassion for the world down to the very depths of its lostness. And also of the wideness of the Church's ministry of diakonia and its implied concern for the totality as well as for the wholeness of human life.

It seems not exaggerated to suggest that in the future it may become the habit to treat of Christ and the Church's participation in and with Him, under the heading of the *munus quintuplex*, in which diakonia is the basic and over-arching category in this dispensation "between the times".

ALL ARE STAMPED WITH THE SEAL

We repeat now in regard to the ministry of diakonia of the Church, as it has been sketched in the preceding pages, what has been said in regard to the missionary being and calling of the Church. It applies to the whole Church, to all its members. All the members are baptized, so to speak, into or stamped with this "diaconal" seal and should acknowledge it with heart and mind. Just as with the missionary aspect, this has to stand as a basic affirmation. It is equally indicative as well as imperative for what is commonly called the body of the "ministry" and for the laity. If this is true (and it seems irrefutably so in looking in the New Testament, in spite of the various shades of structure of Church life), then it is misleading and artificial to reserve or rather to restrict the name "ministry" only to the body of workers that does its work in the direct service of the Church as an institution or organization. The New Testament in speaking about priests and priestly offerings, about diverse forms of diakonia, means always the "saints", one of the most common names of the members of the Christian brotherhood. It has already been observed how scrupulously Paul, a man of strong will and temperament, under the discipline of Christ, respected the integrity and freedom in Christ of the Churches, and nevertheless (not in spite of this respect but as a demonstration that it was not a respect for a worldly, democratic kind of autonomy of the Churches, but for the Christonomy which bound him and the Churches alike) took the liberty of criticizing and reprimanding them forcefully. In his

Church Dogmatics[1] Karl Barth too has summed up the life of every man, but especially the existence of the Church, in a vigorous and imposing way under the word *Dienst* (service).

The Church then as a whole being ministry or diakonia, it follows that, theologically speaking, the ministry of the laity is as constituent for the true being and calling of the Church as the ministry of the "ministry" (the office-bearers or clergy). Both, the ministry of the clergy and the ministry of the laity, are *facts* inherent in the Church's being, are divine data. Only from this angle has the present much-used expression "the ministry of the laity" real content, and is not a mere pious phrase. And more than that. The laity has this calling, this ministry as its indelible character. On this basis one not only *can* but *must* appeal to the laity in order to remind them of their true state. In this view of the God-given ministerial character of the Church as a whole, whether in regard to the clergy or in regard to the laity, there is no question of having "rights". There are different forms and possibilities of diakonia, there are different callings and spheres of diakonia. In 1 Cor. 12 the right orientation has been given in some brief sentences. There are varieties of gifts (*charismata*) but the same Spirit. There are varieties of diakonia but the same Lord. There are varieties of workings of power (*energèma*) but the same God who works everything in everyone. The manifestation of the Spirit is given for the common good. In principle there are no rights. The question of right and status, which necessarily arises when the Church becomes also an organization, has its proper place only

[1] IV/2, pp. 695-825 and III/4, pp. 538 ff. and 683 ff. in German edition.

if it has its first and last motivation in the mutual diakonia, in the *koinonia* in and with Christ. As " right " and as " status " it is secondary, because the whole of the Church is a Christocratic brotherhood. No person, no corporation can have a right or power *vested* in them. For the common good, persons or corporations can have rights or powers *entrusted* to them, under the obedience to the Lordship of Christ the Pantokrator. The searching eye of Christ Pantokrator, to be found in the centre of the top-ceiling in Byzantine Churches, is an awe-inspiring expression of this fact.[1]

THE TRUE MEANING OF LAITY

We can now pursue the remark in Chapter 2 on the derivation of the term " laity " from " laïkos ", which means belonging to the " laos ", the people, i.e. the people of God.

The word " laos " is, in the sense of people of God, applied to Israel in order to express God's special relation to this people. In the New Testament it has the meaning of the people of God composed of Gentiles and Jews. Strictly speaking " laïkos " does not appear in the Bible, but its meaning is clear : pertaining to the " laos ", the people of God. It is a title of honour. We have already dealt with the deplorable development which opposed the " laos ", the " plebs ", the laity, to the priesthood : a development which has its beginnings as early as the end of the first century. The

---

[1] In books on the Ministry this would, it seems, imply a great change. The general plan of these books ought to be : the Ministry of the Church as incumbent on the whole body, specified subsequently by a treatment of the Ministry of the Clergy and of the Ministry of the Laity, always keeping in mind their co-existence and inter-existence.

"laos" means then in the first place the worshipping community. The title of honour, of evidence of divine grace, becomes more and more a title of subordination. But the point we want to make here is that this title of the "people of God" for the Church as a whole is very significant for the understanding of the Church. In the Old Testament it is taken very seriously in regard to Israel. The main passages are Ex. 19:4-7; Deut. 4 and Deut. 7:6-12.

This relation to God rests on a divine covenant, a divine act of election. This act of election *created* Israel as a people, and had nothing to do with qualities inherent in this small, unimportant people itself. The core of the history of Israel is the dramatic contest between God and this people. It constantly transgresses the Covenant, and as constantly it is called back. The Covenant is an allegiance of mutual loyalty and love, to which God keeps, and even in its disloyalty it remains therefore God's people.

In the New Testament the term is applied to the Christian community, Gentiles and Jews. Just as in the Old Testament, God's election stands at the beginning (Eph. 1:3-10 very emphatically). The Christians have as names: saints (Israel's obligation in the Covenant was to be a "holy people") called (*klètoi*). The Church is a community of "called" out of the world (*ekklèsia*). I Peter 2:9 is the classical passage in this respect (you are the elect race, the holy people, the royal priesthood). Just as in the Old Testament Yahweh wanted Israel as His Holy People, i.e. the people which fully acknowledges its belonging to *Him*. It is the same with the Church.

The laos-conception of the Church is deeply embedded in the epistolary part of the New Testament.

It impresses one as not simply being a striking image or symbol. It is rooted in the indissoluble connection between Israel and the Church. Undoubtedly, the mere use of the phrase: "the Church is the people of God" is not particularly helpful, because it remains then often a convenient theological formula, which seems magical but has no real effect. Nevertheless, it is in the heart of the biblical Message and has implications of the greatest importance. Particularly in the present condition of Christendom, and especially in the West with its long history moulded by Christian influences, where one thinks and talks glibly about "Christian peoples", the realization that the Church can never identify itself with any nation is very necessary. We are living in a time in which most Christians live in confusion in regard to their scales of values and priorities. Many honest Christian people experience the shock of a revelation when they are brought to realize that their membership of the Church constitutes a loyalty prior to their loyalty to the nation to which they belong. Patriotism is one of the powerful underground pseudo-religions of to-day, not merely nationalism. The fundamental notion that the Christians are a "peculiar people" that never is identical, or even can be, with a people in the biological, national sense of the word, is largely asleep. It can only become awake by a new grasp of the biblical truth that the Church is the "people of God", an elect race, composed of people *out of all nations, transcending* all nations and races. The universal character of the Church is always, in all circumstances and places, prior and superior to its embodiment within the given nation. This fundamental characteristic has in ordinary Church-life, however, little influence. At best it is a passing

Sunday-feeling. Barth is therefore right in saying: "Sie kann nicht Kirche des Volkes, sondern nur Kirche für das Volk, sie kann nur in diesem Sinne 'Volks- kirche' sein wollen."[1] Our titles betray us: Church of England, *of* Sweden, etc. They reflect a forgetting of the "people *of God*" character of the Church. The only legitimate title for a Church is: Church of Christ *in* . . . The laos-conception of the Church, i.e. of a primarily supernational, superracial body, united around one Lord, throws also a new light on the imperative need of the Ecumenical Movement. In its light disunity is a civil cold war in the Church.

The usual conception of the *Volkskirche* (people's church), comprising the "Christian nation", has inevit- ably driven the Church in the direction of being mainly an institution of worship and of more or less successful education of its members. Since the *corpus christi- anum* idea broke down, this *Volkskirche*-conception has in principle become impossible. At present it is not only in principle but in fact impossible, although there are still Churches which continue to play with this fiction. The Church, big or small, however, should always be aware of being a Church *for, on behalf of,* the people in the midst of which it functions. Let us, however, be grateful to modern secularism, which forces the Church back from historically-grown posi- tions to its fundamental realities. One of these funda- mental realities is that the Church is "the people of God" in Christ. The Churches as they now exist, although in most cases no *Volkskirchen*, nevertheless, just as the old *Volkskirchen*, are mixed Churches,

[1] "The Church cannot be a Church of the people, but only a Church for the people, and only in this sense a 'people's Church'." *Op. cit.* III/4, p. 559 in German edition.

representing as well the fellowship of true believers, the *ekklèsia proprie dicta*, as the merely external community, the *ekklèsia large dicta*. In modern terms we would say: the Church as a spiritual reality and as a sociological phenomenon. Yet we must have the courage and the faith to appeal to this two-faced Church as being and as being called to represent " the people of God ", instead of adjusting and accommodating to its mixed character. To remind the Church, as she empirically is, of her true nature and dignity, of being the dimension where the new world of Christ breaks into the old world, is the only adequate way of raising the summons of the renewal of the Church through repentance and ever new obedience. The essential nature of the Church has incessantly to be presented and interpreted in various tones to the *whole* membership, for only then the right division of light and dark becomes manifest, and the response can be continually purged. In this light it is relevant to insist that the whole membership of the Church is primarily laïkos (lay). Not for the sake of giving to the so-called laity an eminent exalted status, but for the sake of starting from the ground which is common to the whole body; that is to say, to be the " laos " of God.

In so doing in regard to the phrase: the Church is the people of God, nothing different is done from what is done when saying: the Church *is* Mission, or, the Church *is* Ministry (diakonia). Everybody knows that the Church, as she empirically is, is often far from missionary or ministerial in the deep sense which has been outlined above. But the surest and soundest way to help the Church to become truly missionary and ministerial, is to remind her of what she really *is*.

Finally, there must be added a very essential thing. The Church is not only the people of God, but the *expectant* people of God. The band of people which is in the first place forward looking, not backward. Forward to the kingdom of God, to the coming King. And so the people of hope. All service is service to this kingdom. The "people of God" is ruled in the first place by its future, and not by its past or present.

THE LAITY'S RESPONSIBLE SHARE

In the development of our thesis: the Church *is* Ministry (diakonia) and therefore ministry is incumbent on the Church as a whole and not only on a special and specialized body of people "set apart" for the ministry, we have strongly stressed "the ministry of the laity" as an *integral* part of the Church's life and service. *All* members of the ekklèsia have in principle the same calling, responsibility and dignity, have their part in the apostolic and ministerial nature and calling of the Church. Because they live by the same divine grace, all as children and servants of God. "*We* are the Lord's whether we live or die" (Rom. 14:8) says Paul to the whole congregation of Rome. By the nature of the case, this is no "right" or "status" to confide in, but the manner in which the Church manifests the new reality and the new dimension of life, which have become actual in Christ and the presence of the Holy Spirit.

I have said up to now, strictly speaking, nothing which has not been said by others. The only new thing, perhaps (and this seems to me very important), is the insistence on the laity's full, responsible share in bringing the nature and calling of the Church to expression, and their belonging integrally in the doctrine of the Church. A doctrine of the Church which ignores or by-passes it in using generalities, is incomplete and crippled. This amounts to saying that all our historic ecclesiologies are crippled.

This insistence is, in the interest of the Church as a whole *and in the interest of the laity*, which largely ignores it as well, extremely necessary. If this is not done with persevering monotony, the danger is very great indeed that all the talk about a theology of the laity will in the long run remain an *ad hoc* construction to underpin, in theological terms, the so-called contribution which the laity can make in a time like ours, when the Church in its present perplexity and predicament needs the laity so badly. Most lay people are quite satisfied with the " contributory " place accorded them, because they have never thought about their *true* place nor have ever been encouraged to think in that line. Nearly all expositions on the Church are magnetically attracted to the treatment of the place and function of the ordained ministry, whereas the laity as the complementary part either remains out of sight or the view of the Church becomes too laicized. The treatment of the place and function of the ordained ministry is quite in order, because they have indeed their own important place and function; but the reticence on the laity shows the one-sidedness.[1]

[1] A striking example of this magnetic attraction towards the ordained ministry is T. F. Torrance's book: *Royal Priesthood*. The more striking, because the basic assumption in this book, full of profound remarks, is that all that has to be said about the Church regards the Church *as the whole Body*, but the real purpose of the book turns out to be to define a " corporate " conception of the ordained Ministry. The other sector of " the Body ", viz. the laity,

This brief outline of an understanding of the Church as framework and basis for a theology of the laity is, of course, very incomplete. It was intended only to indicate the bare essentials. The way usually followed in formulating an understanding of the nature of the Church is to discuss the *notae ecclesiae*, the oneness, holiness, catholicity and apostolicity of the Church, the Word and the Sacraments. As to the self-evident centrality of the Word and the Sacraments, I have made my position clear in the preceding chapter. As to the other *notae*, oneness etc., they certainly do afford splendid opportunity for important theological reflection, but rarely lead to what I prefer (instead of " notae " or marks) to call " the appropriate reasons and modes of existence " of the Church: *missio, diakonia*. In Christ, God's out-reach to the world has become flesh and blood. Through and in the Church this has to become manifest, and therefore its proper reasons and modes of existence are: *missio* and *diakonia*.

These reasons and modes of existence have and must have their inalienable and basic place in every doctrine of the Church, because they reflect the apostle-ship and diakonos-ship of Christ. And it is rather in the perspective of the Church's meeting her natural partner and opposite, the world, that the true and indispensable place and responsibility of the laity as part of the Church emerges as the much-forgotten, but nevertheless self-evident, aspect of the totality of

vanishes out of sight. It is an excellent performance of thorough " professional " theology, but I regret to say that, with all its pro-fundity and thoroughness, it serves mainly to widen and synthesize two doctrines of Church and Ministry (Anglican and Presbyterian) but does not really strike out in a new dynamic way to take " the *whole* Body ", in its full weight, seriously.

the Church. It seems timely to express the ardent wish that the ecumenical multilogue in "Faith and Order", in its endeavours to arrive at a new christo- and pneumatocentric conception of the Church, should take very seriously into its considerations the "reasons and modes of existence" of the Church and define *expressis verbis* the organic place of the laity as part of the people of God in the Church. E. Schlink says it succinctly in an article in *Kerygma und Dogma* (1957): "Die Kirche als das durch Christus aus der Welt herausgerufene Gottesvolk; die Kirche als das von Christus in die Welt hinausgesandte prophetisch-priesterlich-königliche Volk."[1]

If this does not happen and all the present prophesying about the missionary and ministry character of the Church is in fact treated as a congeries of interesting marginal remarks, unworthy to produce any substantial change in our existing doctrines of the Church, the great opportunity for a fearless self-revision and a truly new self-understanding is missed. The too exclusive concentration on the Church as a worshipping, preaching and sacramental institution will not then get its much-needed correction and reorientation by the stress on the Church's reason and proper mode of existence: *missio, diakonia*.

Although I have often used the term "the whole body", I have on purpose avoided speaking in terms of "the Body of Christ". This image has undoubtedly some prominence in the New Testament, but in the present ecumenical discussion on the Church it is far too confidently assumed as the dominant one, even as

[1] "The Church as the people of God called out from the world through Christ; the Church as the prophetic, priestly, royal people sent forth into the world by Christ."

the only relevant one.[1] How far this is removed from the truth appears very clearly in the interesting document prepared by Paul S. Minear for the World Council of Churches. He has found more than 80 different terms in which the New Testament speaks of the Church, which he rubricates under 20 categories. Some of his conclusions are that the profusion of vocabulary indicates the dangers implicit in selecting any one term (e.g. the Church, the Body of Christ) as a fixed starting-point or as the pivot of all thought, and that all the images used are often interrelated. Minear's document proves at any rate that the rich variety of images and terms must lead to a new probing into " the mysterious reality of the new humanity and the redeemed society ", which is the creation of Christ and His Spirit. Our presentation is, as stated before, avowedly incomplete, but focused on the relation of Church and world, in which the laity is the spearhead.

[1] This must be said also after the appearance of J. A. T. Robinson's *The Body*, which although written mainly from the point of view of meeting the modern situation of the socialized mass-man by a Pauline anthropology, as the writer sees it, contributes also to what might be called in regard to ecclesiology the body-obsession or fascination.

Chapter 6

POSTLUDE

No endeavour has been made to find a non-objectionable definition for the laity, or the word "lay". For our purposes it is clear that it can only be understood in the sense (which sounds inevitably negative, and therefore always causes so much dissatisfaction) of the huge majority of the membership of the Church, which does not belong to the ordained ministry. We include here that new, constantly increasing, group of laymen and lay-women which goes by the name of camouflaged ecclesiastic or clericalized lay people, who move often more than the bulk of the members of the Church in the bemoaned secluded "world of the Church" and have little experience of the dilemmas of *the* world, in the context of which most of the ordinary laity fulfil their function or earn their living. Acknowledging fully the danger of the "clericalized laity" (which certainly increases the more the apparatus of the Churches and various Christian organizations grows in size) they are included on purpose. For the last ten years (since Amsterdam 1948) many people have rightly hammered on the theme that the decisive rôle of the laity is played in the field of what is called the Church-world relationship.[1]

Yet it would stultify the serious intent of a "theology of the laity" if the "clericalized lay" were practically excluded and relegated to the status of an indefinable

[1] The Consultation of the World Council of Churches, held July 15-20, 1957, on "the Renewal of the Church" at Yale Divinity School, treated it as one of the main centres of the discussion.

hybrid third " genus ". They should be claimed as laity or be ordained. The existence of the secluded " world of the Church " with its separate introvert sacral sphere, estranged from the true realities of the day-to-day world, is a very lamentable fact. It is one of the necessary consequences of " a theology of the laity " to break through a seclusion which is unnatural (i.e. contrary to the nature and calling of the Church). It should, however, be noted that this secluded " world of the Church " is heavily secularized in spirit. The " clericalized laity " in the sense of the body of men and women who have their gainful occupation or function in the service of the ecclesiastical apparatus, should be, on the basis of the place and responsibility of the laity, the first to realize that and help to unveil the unnatural and improper alliance of " sacred " and " secular " in which the " world of the Church " lives.[1] The paradoxical situation in which the " world of the Church " finds itself is that on the one hand it has to purge itself from much insidious secularization or worldliness, and on the other hand has to become really worldly, i.e. open to the world and its real concerns and perplexities. In other words, it has to become in a new way un-worldly and worldly in one. The " clericalized lay-groups " should become aware of the great rôle they have to play in this respect.

THE LAITY'S INALIENABLE MINISTRY

The main reason, however, why this group should be included fully in the laity and in the scope of a " theology of the laity " as the best way to overcome the evident danger inherent in their position, is that a

[1] Of course, the clergy have here as stringent a duty.

166

"theology of the laity" is nothing or only an interesting play of theological thinking if it does not truly reflect a real constituent factor of the Church's whole being, inherent in and given with its nature and calling. As has been emphasized in the preceding chapter more than once, the laity, its place, its responsibility, its ministry is as essential an aspect of the Church as that of the clergy. The laity should therefore in principle never be appealed to with the request to be so kind and goodwilling as to help the Church (nobody thinks of speaking in such a way to the ministry or clergy), but simply on the basis of *what they are* by the nature and calling of Christ's Church as the "people of God", sent into the world for witness and service. The peculiar position of the laity is that, living and moving in the context of the day-to-day world, and having literally to serve two masters and to live in two worlds (and here the "clericalized laity" belongs too), they have to affirm their divinely-ordained part as members of the Church, in an ever new decision of first loyalty to the Uppermost Master. Even because of this peculiar position of the laity, the main part of the ministry of the clergy should be to enable the laity to fulfil their peculiar, inalienable ministry. Only, if conceived and understood in this way, a "theology of the laity" is a serious business, and not merely a more or less captivating diversion of thought.

But, although a "theology of the laity" is necessary and indispensable for undergirding and directing a more faithful expression of what the Church is and what the Church is for, it would be unsatisfactory to leave it at that. So in this Postlude we have some observations to offer on *what* has to be undergirded, *for what* there have to be directives (in Germany the better word *Weisung* is used. Better because it has rich biblical undertones and by-tones). The situation and task which opens up then before our eyes is awful and baffling. Everyone, who knows a little of the world in which we live and in which the Church has to carry on its great divine mandate of being the Church of *Christ*, realizes this immediately. It ought to be stated that just because of the unique and unprecedented situation through which we live, utterly different from the structures and conditions in relation to which the Church as an institution, wandering through history, has developed its forms of symbiosis, one-sidedness in stating matters is often inevitable. Moreover, in principle, this one-sidedness should not be feared. Nothing great and new is achieved without one-sided insistence on matters of capital importance. To recognize unprecedented challenges as divine calls, which permanently accompany the Church whether heard or not, is not served best by well-balanced views. These last have of course their significance and value, but by the nature of the case afford too much opportunity for the inertia of historical forces to exercise their restraining influence. The prophets undoubtedly were, humanly speaking, often very one-sided, but it was a one-sidedness in obedient response to a divine command. It is this prophetic one-sidedness which the Christian Church needs to-day, and should earnestly pray for.

In a "theology of the laity", as already observed, are implied consequences of great import towards two sides. Two sides, because the place, the responsibility, the contribution of the laity, both in the Church and in the world, need thorough reconsideration. Particularly in our time for a body which is so strongly historically conditioned as the Church, though it should be emphatically noted that a " theology of the laity " is not only valid and necessary for our time of kaleidoscopic transition, but is *permanently valid* in all times. In times of disturbance and confusion when the Church seems to need its laity desperately, and in times of consolidation and relative stability when the Church does not seem to need its laity. The two sides in regard to which a discovery of consequences has to be made fearlessly are :

1. *The revision of the structure of the Church* as inherited from the past and therefore, according to the sociological law of the propensity of institutions to last, in many respects slow in changing. One should be thoroughly aware of the innate stubbornness of the resistant forces; which need not be ascribed to malevolence, but to blindness and often to a disastrous sacralization of past institutions and attitudes. In the Dutch magazine *Wending*, H. J. Hoekendijk makes the passing remark that the Reformed Church in France treated recently a proposal to alter the liturgy of the Lord's Supper in three consecutive long sessions of the Synod, but found only one morning to discuss superficially the reform of structure. This is a striking illustration of this innate resistance to far-reaching change, or at least to facing it seriously and fearlessly. It is therefore imperative to plead for it with one-sided monotony. The " world of the Church ", in its comparative sacral isolation, cannot be left untouched.

THE LAITY'S UNINTERRUPTED DIALOGUE

2. The fact which characterizes the huge majority of the laity, viz. their being in the world, and their

being dispersed in and through the world, its institutions, enterprises, relationships and pursuits. There is their *locus standi et vivendi*, and therefore their indicated place and working sphere as the laity *of the Church*. For quite a long time there has been much discussion on the point that the Church after a rather long withdrawal has to meet the world again. This has resulted in many pronouncements or pastoral messages from ecumenical bodies as well as from individual Churches, on great topics of the day, touching all the realms of human life. In these pronouncements, amongst which there are many excellent ones, the Church in many places has resumed her teaching responsibility to the Church membership, to the world at large and to the powers that be. Sometimes also her prophetic office. Sometimes, because not all teaching is necessarily prophetic. This is a kind of meeting, of dialogue with the world, which has its due place; and it should be supported by the prayer of its whole membership for the guidance of the Holy Spirit in order that the Church may speak clearly, humbly and appropriately, in the name of Him who came to serve and not to lord it over the world. But if the laity of the Church, dispersed in and through the world, are really what they are called to be, the real uninterrupted dialogue between Church and world happens through them. They form the daily repeated projection of the Church into the world. They embody the meeting of Church and World.

To say this is at the same time to realize the glaring distance between the reality which obtains and the reality to which these simple but tremendous sentences point. To say this is therefore at the same time also to point to the tremendous necessity of a radical change in the Church and not less in the laity themselves. The situation is not that the Church has merely to seize this point and to direct and guide its laity accordingly. As if, so to speak, the laity were simply waiting for a marching-order to move, with determination and discernment. It is, as everybody who is interested knows, quite different. It is, as said already, awful and baffling. It is the greatest issue now before the Church. How to become a Church which daily meets and is in dialogue with the world in its laity. Not because this laity is in itself so excellent, but simply because this is the main reason of the laity's existence as a *Christian* laity, as the people in whom is alive the reality of God's redemptive power and of the expectation of His Kingdom as the order of existence for which the whole world unconsciously yearns (even in its many idealistic endeavours to take it by force). But again in saying this we realize that this seems to be a phantasmagoria, a childish delusion, a "pie in the sky" of a different sort from the doping of an intolerable existence by an illusory compensation of a better life hereafter. And yet, what has been said about the Church's nature and calling and consequently about the laity's nature and calling is the faith through and by which the Christian has to live, if he really knows what the Christian faith is about. It is a matter of "do or die", "behave yourself according to the divine privilege and calling in which you stand and are set, or acknowledge your unbelief".

Why does it seem a phantasmagoria and a delusion? For reasons existing in the Church as she empirically is, and in the laity. To put it sharply in the face of the magnitude of this concern about the true Church-World relationship, we must stop speaking mainly of the reconversion or rechristianization of England or Holland or New York,[1] without speaking with even greater fervency of the reconversion or rechristianization of the Church itself and of its laity, on which we seem to build such great hopes as evangelistic witnesses and faithful "servants". This has to be acknowledged in a spirit of true repentance and humility, because repentance and humility are the primary condition for a truly new start and for the venture of faith to live up, in all weakness and imperfection, to the seeming phantasmagoria. We formulate it in this way to avoid implying that it is first a matter of constructing great daring programmes, full of vision; although to be sure it implies a programme of radical remoulding of the Church itself and of the laity. Repentance and humility have to precede, accompany and underscore the remoulding. If the latter is the direct aim, we commit an inversion of spiritual order, which ends in disaster. It has always to be remembered that Israel is not only the foreshadowing prototype of the Church in its essential traits, but also in its repeated unfaithfulness and false interpretation of its calling.

If the specific place of the laity in the world is at the frontiers, where the real dialogue between Church and World becomes an event, the laity at large needs a new orientation, a new grasp of the whole realm and scale of the reality of Christ, and a new equipment. This holds true also for a great number of faithful Church members, accepting implicitly the Christian Faith as they hear it presented in Church and keeping

[1] This does of course not mean absolutely to stop thinking, speaking and acting about evangelizing the world. What it is trying to say is the simple truth that all good things begin at home.

to the observances, but in fact ignorant in regard to the Christian Faith and its relevance to the world. They are, to borrow a phrase from T. S. Eliot's *The Idea of a Christian Society*, like many people who are neither Christians nor non-Christians, "living in no man's land". The word dialogue has a special relevance. Dialogue means exchange, *mutual* communication. It means give and take, because, alienated as especially our present world may be from the Christian apprehension of man, life and the world, it is a fact that the world has much to teach us. It forces us by its inquisitive spirit of discovery, in which Christians also take part, and by its ingenuous creativity in the midst of chaos in developing great schemes for making life better "livable" and manifesting an impressive multi-form humanitarian responsibility for fellow-men (in which Christians take part too), to reinterpret the Christian Message and to learn again in all humility the lesson that the children of darkness are often wiser than the children of light. Therefore a laity which really fulfils its part in the dialogue cannot and should not pretend to be superior, or pose as guaranteeing by Christianity the solution of all common problems (common to all men, wherever they stand) or the sweeping reform of society, but should simply and unpretentiously be a peculiar salt and spread light or illumination by helping themselves and the world to put the right questions.

Being in dialogue with the world, being dispersed in the world as representing the Christian Church in its disturbing and healing quality, is foremost a matter of *being* and not of *doing*. This does not mean, of course, that doing does not matter. Far from that. Doing matters very much, and the kind and spirit of doing also; but being is prior. In putting it in this way, we do not propose an artificial and non-existent either-or, but keep to the maxim that first things should be first. A remarkable word, which gives the right sense of direction, is 1 Cor. 15:58: "*Therefore*, my beloved brethren, be ye steadfast, unmovable, always abounding in the work of the Lord, forasmuch as ye know that your labour is not in vain in the Lord." The verse begins with "therefore". Consequently we must ask: why is that? Because "therefore" points to the resurrection of "our Lord Jesus Christ" in whom the victory *is* already assured. Therefore the Christian can and should work abundantly in serving the Lord, for in Him the labour is never "in vain". Being in the Lord and *His* victory is primary. The natural fruit is abundant work, not for the sake of *our* victory, but as expression of our sense of direction, which is serving Christ by serving others.

Christians can therefore never pose or present themselves as the Savers of the world. They are no more nor less than the servants of the Saviour and Redeemer.

If our subject were to answer the question whether, in the present world of servitudes to economic and power-politics necessities with all that these servitudes include, it is possible for a Christian to live as a Christian in the world, the answer would be: there are a certain number of individual Christians who, by the grace of God, do so. But we cannot leave it at that. Our subject is still more exacting, viz. how is it possible to minister to the laity as a whole in such a way that it can fulfil its destiny and live as *a Christian laity* in the world of to-day? If we do not put the matter in this uncompromising way, all talk about the specific and decisive rôle of the laity in the dialogue with the world is hollow. On the other hand it is clear that the laity, as an organic part of the Church and its representative in the world, needs the help of the Church. Not as a haven of refuge, which is in most cases another form of escapism, of letting the world go to the devil. But as the nourishing and understanding mother, the community which by prayer, sacrament and ways of true fellowship (*koinonia*) sustains its members in the battle.

In saying this we are immediately confronted with another baffling question. Baffling because it can by no means be maintained that the Church in its usual run is so realistically and passionately bent on the perplexities of life in the world of to-day that it is able to be such a nourishing, sustaining, guiding, rebuking and understanding mother. Many lay members, men and women, who in all sincerity wage their warfare out of obedience to Jesus Christ, have had the experience that the Church as such leaves him (or her) alone in his (her) dispersion, often counting them rather unprofitable, unfaithful members, because they do not figure in the apparatus of the Church nor desire to do so. Baffling also because it sometimes seems hopeless to make "the closed world of the Church" perform the complete somersault of becoming an open Church, that is to say a place from whose centre, the Holy Meal of fellowship with and in Christ, and so with each other, all ways go straight into the streets and byways of the world. For the word of the elder Blumhardt that every Christian needs two conversions: first to Christ and then to the world, can still help us to see the problem in its simplicity and depth.

In asking these questions we are led back again to the revision of the structure of the Church, which is a colossal thing, because it involves liberation from the burden of history.

THE FROZEN CREDITS OF THE CHURCH

In all our criticism and sometimes near-despair of the institutional Church, it should never be forgotten that many powers and possibilities really exist in it, but often in captivity; exist as frozen credits and dead capital. The truth of this statement is proved by the many signs of renewal and reshapement about which we have spoken. Sometimes they are wrested from a recalcitrant institutional Church, sometimes they find understanding and support. But even if the latter case is true, it is still far removed from what should be meant by a revision of the structure of the Church as it is implied in a "theology of the laity", its presuppositions and its consequences. Sometimes, unconcerned about recalcitrance or support, all kinds of new initiative, leaping out of the bonds of captivity, surge up, make their way and exercise their infectious influence. All such lay-movements and experiments, often led and supported by members of the Ministry, are pioneering forerunners. To a great extent they tend to happen more outside the walls than inside. There are amongst the lay-movements some which simplify and (what is more serious) falsify the problem by making their aim the increase of Church membership, implicitly assuming that the Church as a whole is quite in order. Although not saying so in express terms, they act and execute their programmes with the unspoken presupposition that the churchification of the world is its salvation. Without realizing it, the Church as well as the world is left unaltered.

But, if one thing is clear as soon as the Church becomes serious about its missionary and ministerial calling for the world, it is that two difficult roads in
particular have to be trodden. First, the road towards
overcoming the scantiness of its knowledge of the world
of to-day, and its ignoring of what really goes on in the
world under the surface. Secondly, the road towards
reforming its spirit, atmosphere and inherited structure
in so far as they give no room for new vitality.

It is impossible to enter into any detailed discussion
of what such a revision of the structure of the Church
concretely means. It has to be different according to
the various inherited structures and the very different
environments in which they function. What can and
must be said and resaid, with all gratitude for what in
many places is already happening, is that a fearless
scrutiny and revision of structure is one of the most
urgent aspects of a renewal of the Church. It must be
said and resaid even with irritating insistence, because
the Church as institution is one of the hardest nuts to
crack. Like all institutions, worldly or religious, the
Church is on its institutional side most resistant. In
many respects Churches are more recalcitrant to change
than any other institution, because they have sacralized
themselves.

WHAT NEW WAYS?

The directives for this self-revision are:

First, along what ways is it possible to express in
new forms of fellowship and community the fact
(which is now rarely evident) that the Church is a
Christocratic fraternity? In doing this a greater act
of evangelism would be done than all evangelistic cam-

paigns together, and even more. It would mean demonstrating its authenticity. How do we break through the sociological imprisonment which is so often spoken about? It is deeply distressing to undergo so often the experience that our so-called "beautiful services" result more in being a dope than a tonic. E. R. Wickham's book *Church and People in an Industrial City* (1957) not only strikes in my opinion the right note, but also shows the right way to acquire that new understanding of the causes of the inevitable dechristianization of modern society and of the Church's impotence to meet it, and a new self-understanding of the Church.

Second, how can the laity be given a greater participation in the worship (liturgy and preaching), in the teaching function, and in the "ruling" of the Church? This would mean a constant alertness to the diversity of gifts which exists, but does not find expression.

Third, especially in this time of mobility and rapid social change, a great flexibility and readiness for decentralization is required. A great openmindedness to the insight into, and knowledge of, the environment in which the Church has to perform its apostolic witness and diakonia in the world, as provided by sociological investigation, is indispensable. What is called secularism is not only apostasy (most people don't know apostasy, because they have never known faith) but a legitimate and, by its results, largely justified claim to use our human resources for solving our human problems. Outstanding traits of modern society are loneliness and massification. Both belong together. They imply an irrepressible drift towards virtual or actual nihilism, inner emptiness and loss of real sense of direction. The direct approach to these deep-seated diseases has no great promise, because the de-religionizing of vast sectors of people in modern society has deep-seated and long-range historical causes.

The indirect approach by really *being* communities of mutual upbuilding, of witness and service, by building in the desert of modern life genuine Christian cells, is the one indicated. Because it reveals a new Christian ethos. Words like reconversion or rechristianization of a dechristianized environment always suggest involuntarily a grandiose, spectacular undertaking. The way of the Church as the body that has the mandate to express the ministry of the great *Diakonos* is not spectacular. The "first fruits" of fraternities, house-churches, para-parochial congregations, retreats (not for retreat's sake, but for the sake of going out into the world) etc. should not continue to exist alongside the Church. They should be acknowledged as really doing *the* business of the Church, also the institutional Church. All these pioneer movements should not be left to the imaginative inventiveness of those individuals who took the initiative, but adventuring in these directions should become also the concern of the Churches, because they are reminders of what the Church really exists for. The Church cannot aim at conquering, but must aim at interpenetrating the world and so communicating with it. The way for the institutional Church to get into the stream is, it seems, to confront incessantly the official local congregations, whether in urban, suburban, middle-town or rural environment, with a simple question. What does it involve to be a Christocratic brotherhood? Not a place where religion of a certain brand brings people together at stated times for stated activities, but a brotherhood where everybody finds his or her place, as in 1 Cor. 12, and where the creative fact is the living Christ, the

Redemer and Reconciler, who wants to reach the world to minister to it through His redeemed. For the world wants to *see* redemption. It is not interested in being talked to about it.

It is certain that in the light of a searching question like this the ecumenical question would immediately become a burning one, not on theoretical considerations but because to be a Christocratic brotherhood effects immediately an illegitimate and hypocritical pretension if it does not throw us together. There cannot be at one place more than one Christocratic fraternity, though often functioning in many groupings, for the Lord who reigns (*kratein*) is one and indivisible.

It is a blessing that at present through the World Council of Churches and some of its agencies there has been created a possibility of mutual communication between all the pathfinding activities done on the long road towards the renewal of the Church. It creates an ever increasing stimulus and pressure, which needs must have their effect on that most difficult of citadels, the institutional Church, hardened in its historic shell. But the great step towards recovery of the integrity and authenticity of the Church as a Christocentric and Christocratic brotherhood is the unreserved recognition of the essential part of the laity in the expression of the Church's peculiar mode of being, and of the elementary fact that in the Church *everybody* has the apostolic and ministerial "office" (*Amt*), whether he or she is ordained minister or not. The point we can't evade is that, true as it may be that for many important historical reasons the Church has become from a charismatic fellowship an institutional Church, she must acknowledge that, as to her *nature*, she is *always* charismatic, for she is the working field of the Holy

Spirit. Her being an institution is a human necessity, but not the nature of the Church. Our latent but very acute difficulty is that we do not really believe it. We live by the unavowed idea that the Church *is* an institution, has been once (in a so-called "ideal" early period) charismatic, and sometimes still can show signs of its charismatic character. In fact, the Church leaves it to the "Sects" to entertain this "idealistic illusion". And yet the Sects, in spite of our justified criticisms of their usual behaviour and misinterpretation of the biblical meaning of the Church as a charismatic brotherhood, are right. The charismatic nature of the Church as an abiding basic fact, and not as a passing stage, has to be affirmed with deep conviction. That does not mean that she must always be filled by striking phenomena as discussed e.g. in 1 Cor. 12-14 as spiritual gifts. But the Church should consciously affirm its charismatic above its institutional nature. Otherwise we deny unintentionally that the Holy Spirit is the Church's truly vivifying power. It is very noteworthy that 1 Cor. 12, which presents so clearly the charismatic nature of the Church, in which all the members in particular find their place and part, without any ado (vs. 28) puts in the list of charismatic offices the "helpers and administrative governments".

THE LAITY IS THE DISPERSION OF THE CHURCH

Finally we must return to the Church-World relationship in which the laity, by the fact of its living in the world, plays a more decisive rôle than the clergy can. If the significance of the laity means, as is maintained throughout in our exposition, the dispersion of the

Church through the laity in the world, then the basic observation has to be made that the Church in its being and calling is a unity of opposites: it is antithetical to the world and yet bound to it by infinite commitment. Our Lord Jesus Christ, at the moment when He was on His way to the Cross for the reconciliation of the world, said to Pilate: "My kingdom is not of this world." The Church-World relationship has to be conceived in the context of that personalist, relational, religious thinking, which is peculiar to the Bible. God, Christ, the Holy Spirit are "Thou's" and "I's", not a sacred or sacral sphere as is the case in the category of sacred-secular or spiritual-temporal. The central fact of the Christian life is the primacy of one's allegiance to Jesus Christ, the living Lord above all other allegiances. Because of that allegiance the life of the Christian is committed to the ministry of the world in its needs and anxieties and triumphs.

In looking at the biblical witness it appears impossible to put the Church-World relationship in a simplistic way. The Old Testament strikes a strong positive note. The world is God's creation and remains His world, His concern, also after the break between Him and mankind as represented in Adam. "The earth is the Lord's and the fullness thereof." The fierce denunciations of the prophets are the strongest positive affirmations of God's Lordship over all life-structures. Man is dependent on God's Lordship and therefore accountable to Him, but relatively autonomous and independent, because man has received a mandate "to have dominion" and has to express his ultimate and basic dependence and accountability through *voluntary* obedience. Although there are notions of sacred and profane in the Old Testament, they are overruled by the basic distinction of God the Lord, and man, the obedient or disobedient, which is a religious-ethical distinction. In the New Testament, especially in the Gospel and Epistles of John, there is in the first place a strong negative accent (which the Pietistic view has so exclusively developed), although it must be kept in mind that the Old Testament remains also in this case the background of the New Testament. The world lies "in the Evil", the Head of the world (1 John 4:3; John 15:19; 17:6, 14, 16). The Church does not belong to the world, because the believers are "in Christ", the "new creation". They will have tribulation, but are predestined to be victors (John 17:18; John 16; 1 John 5:4, 5). In the epistolary exhortations there is a distinct tone of aloofness, of keeping "unspotted". The Christians are "pilgrims" and "sojourners" (Hebrews). On principle, they are not at home in the world.

Yet these negative tones are combined with clearly positive tones. The world is the theatre and the purpose of the divine drama of redemption. It is God's world and the object of His concern. The disciples are called to be the salt and light of the world. Jesus Himself is entering fully into the world's physical and spiritual distress. He dies for the world. He is the centre of human history, the sole Hope of the world. He reconciles the world to God, is its King and Judge, and leads it to renewal. This dialectical relationship of Church and World, this polar combination of antithesis and full commitment to the world, gives *in principle* the true picture. In principle, because it needs to be added that the Church in her empirical, historical manifestation has belonged often to the "world" in the sense of lying "in the Evil". This indicates already that according to biblical categories one can do little with such terms as the Church as the " sacred ".[1] In Christ, the suffering Servant, the Church is not the sphere of the sacred, but the world of the forgiven sinners and of the servants of Him who came to serve the world.

This polar combination of antithesis to and of self-surrendering solidarity with the world belongs to her divine being and calling in order to manifest the mystery of Christ in the world. It implies that this peculiar kind of Christ's deep solidarity with the world points to a Church-World relationship which is a category of its own, breaking through the usual categories of sacred-secular, spiritual-temporal. The category " sacred "-secular (profane) is by origin and meaning pagan, pointing to a realm of an awe-inspiring and dangerous substance or force, and the profane where this is absent. In the history of the Christian Church the categories sacred-secular (profane) or spiritual-temporal have served to express claims of dominion and power of the sacred (spiritual) over the other. In the Church-World relationship as we have tried to express it the Church stands to the world in a relationship of service and witness; as a reflection of Christ, its Head, the Apostle and *Diakonos* to the world. Church and World are both God's but each in a peculiar sense. The Church as the " purchased possession " (Eph. 1 : 14; Hebr. 9 : 15; Acts 20 : 28) and the " earnest of the Kingdom ". The world as God's creation, man's working-place to manifest the partner-

[1] A remarkable passage for the abolition of the sacred-secular or sacred-profane distinction is Peter's declaration in Acts 10. In vs. 28 he says the tremendous words : " God has shown me that I must not call any man common or unclean." Cf. also vs. 15. Common=profane.

ship with God in dominion over the creation, and the domain claimed as theatre of the fulfilment of God's will (Matthew 6:10).

On the background of a theology *of* the laity, the indispensable complement is to develop various theologies of the realities and spheres of the world[1] for the Church and *for* the laity. In recent years the cry for a theology of society, of work, of the common life, of money, of property—to mention only a few—is raised. The important thing in this cry is that in it becomes manifest the realization that at the present time the Church is inescapably confronted with the demand of a total rethinking of the relevance of the Christian Message to the present world. The same realization stirs behind the demand for a new, relevant Christian ethic (individual and social). This immediately follows from the focal point in the Church-World relationship, viz. that it has to be witness and service. Witness through service. Service through witness. And witness and service both are service of Christ. It is essential to see this in its full compass, because it implies the combination of commitment to the world and independence from it.

THE CHURCH IS AN INTERFERING COMMUNITY

Another way of saying the same thing is that the Church to-day has to become determined to learn a new way of talking to the world and not less of interfering with the world. A new way of talking, because the secularized world in which we live has developed

[1] On the Roman Catholic side G. Thils has published under this angle: *Théologie des réalités terrestres.*

so many new, human possibilities that she can only be legitimately talked to if she is also *listened* to, and the talking has a chance of becoming real *mutual* communication. A new way of interfering, because in the first place it is appalling to notice the smallness of the Church's significance in the welter of the dominant powers and tendencies which govern men's lives and thinking. The religious boom in America, for instance, does not alter this fact in the slightest. The modern world, by its victorious secularism, has domesticated the Church into a "reservation" for people with "religious" needs, and the Church has largely accepted this domestication. In the second place, the Church has to learn a new lesson of interfering with the world because our secularized world needs as much a fearless self-scrutiny as to its where and whence as the Church itself. It is the Church's plain calling to help the world in this respect. A new way of *talking* and of *interfering* means nothing else than relevant witness and service in quite new dimensions which have still to be discovered. But this witness and service of the Church is not meant as adjustment to the world, its ways and desires, but as bringing to light its real needs and perplexities.

This talking and interfering, this witness and service, has to express itself therefore in ways that seem contradictory.

Unselfish and disinterested service to fellow-men, in numberless forms, often without uttering one so-called "religious" word; being reconciler in the grievous conflicts that separate men and communities; questioning the world incessantly and inducing it to put the *right* questions in regard to its problems; letting itself be questioned by the world, contradicting it when necessary, and reminding it of the divine judgment which hangs over everything and everyone; throughout all this service, reconciliation, contradiction and questioning sounding the note of the certainty of God's triumphant love.

All these demands for theologies *of* and *for* the laity tend to sound as if the problem of having a laity, which functions as an essential aspect of the Church, were mainly a matter of theological training and schooling. It is not. At any rate, it should not be. To be sure, a staggering amount of intense collaboration between theologians, ministers and laity is absolutely necessary in order to enable the Church and its membership to *speak* with a new voice and *act* with new vigour and vision at the present day. Remoulding the laity involves an equally drastic remoulding of the ministry and of the theologians. All three categories need to place their task and vocation under the light of that profound, revolutionary word: *diakonia*, which is not a merely ethical, humanitarian category but rather the deepest religious category, which lies at the bottom of the Gospel. But the object neither can nor should be to make the laity a band of minor theologians. What every member of the Church, of whatever description and condition, needs is Christian enlightenment and spiritual intelligence according to his (or her) needs and possibilities, which is different from theological training.

But this is all of no avail if we, who belong to the Church, are not struck to the roots of our being by the critical and liberating question: is our witness and service really service of Him who became our Servant in order that we might become His Servants? Therefore, a theology of the laity which has as its fundamental basis the exemplary divine diakonia as the only true way to a reform of the Church is not a programme for a new victorious period of the Church, however " abounding in the work of the Lord " she may become. It is a call to readiness for suffering and sacrifice, which is merely a reflection of the suffering and sacrifice of the Great Servant, through whom we know that the love of God burns undyingly in the heart of this seemingly forlorn world.

The last word that has to be said is to repeat the request already directed at the Commission of Faith and Order, which has the main official responsibility for the ecumenical discussion on the Church. The request is: Will you take seriously the essential place of the laity (as essential as that of the clergy) in your work of rethinking the doctrine of the Church or not? If so, this means an important change in the ecclesiological quest. If not, then all talk about a theology of the laity is an interesting intermezzo in the Church's realm of discourse, but in essence it is vain.

INDEX

INDEX